Myths, Mysteries and Legends of Alabama

Elaine Hobson Miller

Seacoast Publishing
Birmingham, Alabama

ISBN 1-878561-44-8

Published by
Seacoast Publishing Inc.
110 12th St. North
Birmingham, AL 35203
(205) 250-8016

Manufactured in the United States of America

Contents

To
DADDY
(the late Elbert A. Hobson)

and to
PAW-PAW
(the late B.E. Edwards),

whose love and patience
were legendary.

Foreword

If you're looking for ghost stories, you've opened the wrong book. The tales between these pages are about the real world, not the supernatural. An eclectic collection, they run the gamut from ancient legends to modern mysteries, beginning with the debate over who discovered America, and ending with the controversy over Sand Mountain's mutilated cows.

Between those extremes, you'll meet a Baldwin County train robber who eluded the law by changing into animal shapes, and a Bessemer prostitute whose corpse refused to decay.

Stories such as the UFO sightings at Fyffe, the disappearance of The Flying Dutchman in the Gulf of Mexico, the famous Jefferson County Dye/Brasher disappearance case and the pecan tree that made a mysterious moaning noise have been reported in bits and pieces in various newspapers. But, to my knowledge, this is the first time each has been pulled together into a cohesive form that tells its entire story from beginning to end.

Some of these tales may be familiar to you, but take unfamiliar twists in this book. You'll learn where the famous contest between John Henry and the steam drill really took place, and the reasoning of Tecumseh, the famous Shawnee warrior-chief, whose ire against an Alabama Indian resulted in a terrible earthquake.

When you meet the unseen beast that terrorized Selma teenagers during the 1950s, and the lawyer who met a gruesome death, you'll be reading anecdotes that, until now, were simply handed down within their respective families.

As the title of this book suggests, some stories are true, while others are based on truth that has been stretched to explain the unexplainable. I refuse to categorize them, but leave it to you, the reader, to make up your own mind as to which is which.

— *Elaine Hobson Miller*
August, 1995

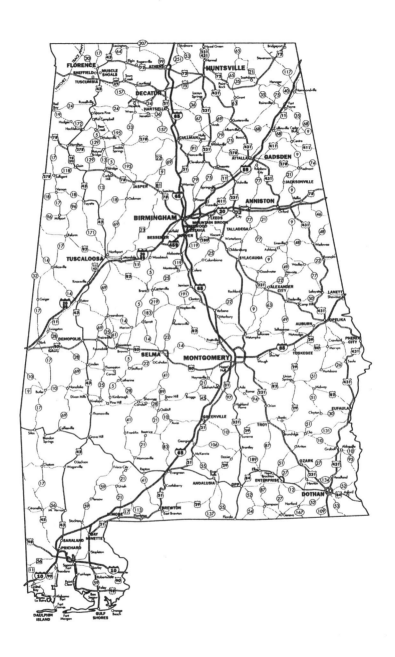

*Were remains of an ancient fort near DeSoto Falls in
northeast Alabama built by the discoverers of America?*

Prince Madoc And The Discovery Of America

"In fourteen hundred and ninety-two, Columbus sailed the ocean blue." Every child who has ever sung that little ditty probably knows the follow-up story of how the first permanent British settlement was established at Jamestown in 1607.

But was it truly the first?

Legend has it that a Welsh prince named Madoc sailed into Mobile Bay in 1170, more than 300 years before Christopher Columbus bumped into the West Indies. No primary evidence exists to substantiate the Madoc story, so many historians relegate it to the level of semi-mysticism afforded King Arthur and his Knights of the Round Table. Yet it caused sufficient distress to European monarchs of the 15th and 16th centuries that England's James I finally labeled it "Tudor propaganda" in order to keep peace with Spain.

If the legend had been accepted as truth, it would have changed the course of world history. Britain would have had first claim on the New World, Columbus's feat would be of secondary importance in the history books, and Alabama's Gulf Shores would replace Jamestown as the true birthplace of the United States.

History documents a Prince Madoc who was one of 17 sons of Owain Gwyneth, ruler of Gwynedd, the northern kingdom of Cambria (now Wales) in 1137. When Owain died in 1169, a violent fight erupted among the heirs to his throne.

An old law stated that only an unblemished king could rule Cambria. That immediately eliminated Jarwarth (Edward), the eldest legitimate son, because of a facial disfigurement. Howell was older than Jarwarth, but Howell was illegitimate, and considered basely born because his mother was Irish.

Nevertheless, Howell claimed the throne and ruled until his mother's death. When he left Cambria to claim his mother's estates in Ireland, his half-brother, Daffyd (David), took over, and killed Howell when the latter returned. Daffyd ruled uncontested until Jarwarth's son, Llewellyn, came of age and claimed his father's kingdom.

Madoc, who probably was illegitimate, too, may have feared for his own safety, because Daffyd had two or three of the brothers killed in his attempts to maintain his hold on the throne. Hearing rumors of a vast new land across the ocean to the west, Madoc set sail in 1170 with an intrepid band of followers.

Steering by the stars and propelled by the prevailing winds and currents, Madoc crossed the Atlantic, sailed up the Gulf of Mexico, and dropped anchor in Mobile Bay.

The land he discovered was lush and green, the fruit and flowers were plentiful, and the climate much to Madoc's liking.

It was better than craggy Cambria, with its family feud and the constant battle against the Normans, who had already conquered the southern Cambrian kingdom of Powys.

Leaving most of the first adventurers behind, Madoc and a handful of crewmen returned to Gwynedd to entice more countrymen to this wild new land. The next year, 1171, he sailed again in his ship, the Gwennon Gorn, accompanied by his brother, Rhyrd, in the Saint Peter. Some stories say that one of his sisters and several other women came along for the ride.

Anti-Madoc historians argue that even if the Welshman had stumbled into the New World, he never could have found his way back to Cambria without the modern compass. But the Vikings used a primitive compass in the form of a needle magnetized by a lodestone floating on a chip in a bowl of water, and Madoc had a Viking ancestor in his lineage. Several ships assembled for Richard I's third crusade, just a few years after Madoc's voyages, were outfitted with such a navigational device, so it is conceivable that Madoc possessed one.

A legend associated with the name of Madoc's ship adds validity to the primitive compass theory. "Gwennon Gorn" means "Horn of the Gwennon," and Gwennon means "stag." Ancient bards told how Madoc designed and built a ship using nails of stag horn because traditional iron nails would have thrown off the magnet of the Icelandic compass.

Madoc probably knew the trade winds and ocean currents that were favorable to such a voyage, too. That's the opinion of Irene Patton Parker, a Florence, Alabama, resident who, though not a professional historian, spent 25 years researching the Madoc legend on both sides of the Atlantic.

"During certain months, the northeast trade winds could carry a ship down past the coast of Spain to Northern Africa, across the Atlantic to the Gulf of

Mexico," Mrs. Parker stated in her 1970 book, *The Welsh Connection*. "The Canary and Equatorial currents followed much the same pattern, so a ship had both current and wind to help make the voyage. Madoc knew how to follow the Gulf Stream up the coast of North America and pick up the Atlantic drift that carried him straight home to the British Isles." She says this information comes from Peter Freuchen's book, *The Seven Seas*.

What happened to Madoc's second party adds further to the mystery, because when he sailed from Cambria the second time, he was never heard from again. Evidence indicates that he encountered storms in the Caribbean and was blown off course.

Here, the legend takes a tributary and sails into muddy waters.

It has been suggested that Madoc beached on the shores of Mexico, where he was dubbed Quetzalcoatl, god of the ancient Aztecs. The Aztecs claimed their god came by sea from the north in a square-sailed ship. In Mexico today, figures of Quetzalcoatl decorating the walls of Aztec temple ruins depict him as a plumed serpent or dragon, a figure that strongly resembles the Red Dragon, the emblem of ancient Cambria.

Even though conclusive proof of Madoc's voyages cannot be found, a mountain of circumstantial evidence has accumulated through the centuries.

The story was first sung in the ballads of the ancient bards. More than simple wandering minstrels who could spin a good yarn, bards were the historians when history was recorded orally.

They were trained in the art of memorization, and there is every reason to believe their songs depicted events that actually happened. During the reign of Edward IV (1451-1483), a highly-respected Welsh bard named Gutyn Owen went beyond memorization and produced a written manuscript called the *Brut Y Twysogion*, which contained the Madoc story.

"In 1589, Richard Hakluyt, historian, for whom the prestigious Hakluyt Society is named, included it (the Madoc saga) in one of his three folio volumes on early English voyages," Irene Parker wrote in *The Welsh Connection.* "Hakluyt took the story from *The History of Cambria*, published two years before by Dr. M. David Powel, Doctor of Letters, who had added Humphrey Lloyd's *Translations and Continuations of Caradoc of Llancarvan*, based on the manuscript written by Gutyn Owen."

Other manuscripts, while not directly connecting Madoc to America, add credibility to his legend. The first, stored today in the British National Museum, London, identifies the kings of Gwynedd and gives the long lineage of the Gwynedd family. Dated 1477, 25 years before Columbus sailed, the manuscript notes that Owain's son was an explorer of "unknown lands."

Parts of another manuscript, entitled "The Romance of Madoc, 1255," were discovered in Poitiers, France, in the 17th century.

Written by a 13th century Flemish writer named Willem the Minstrel, this "Romance" tells the story of Madoc and his discovery of "a Paradise under the sea."

English travelers of the 1500s and 1600s frequently returned home from the New World to report of encounters with Indians whose language bore an amazing similarity to the Welsh tongue.

These reports so shook the Spanish monarchs that they deployed three expeditions to find these possible descendants of Madoc's first voyage.

"In 1557, Parda de Luna was sent up the Mobile and Coosa Rivers to look for the 'gente blanco,'" wrote Irene Parker. "In 1624, they searched further inland as far as the Alabama-Georgia line, close to Chattanooga. They had correct information, for this is the route the Welsh obviously took, but they never found the white men with beards. Each time they had moved further north."

When Spain sent Pierre le Moyne, Sieur d'Iberville, to America to select a site for a town on the Gulf Coast, he founded Mobile in 1711, on a river the local Mobilia Indians called the "Mad Dog" River. It is not inconceivable that ancestors of these Indians named the waterway after Madoc, which was spelled "Madog" in the Welsh tongue. (That body of water is known as Dog River today.)

On this side of the Atlantic, Cherokee legends, the remains of pre-Columbian stone fortifications and further reports of fair-skinned, Welsh-speaking Indians lend credence to the Madoc legend.

In 1810, John Sevier, first governor of Tennessee and an authority on Indians, answered a letter from Major Amos Stoddard regarding his experiences with people who knew of these Welsh Indians. Gov. Sevier had stumbled onto some ancient stone fortifications during his Indian campaigns in Tennessee and Kentucky in 1782. When he met the venerable old Cherokee chief, Oconostoto, he asked whether the chief knew anything about those fortifications.

According to Sevier's letter to Stoddard, Chief Oconostoto recalled stories his forefathers told about how the forts had been built by a white people called "Welsh" who had crossed the ocean and landed first near the mouth of the Alabama river near Mobile. These whites were driven inland until they reached the Hiwassee River just inside today's Tennessee. Oconostoto said his ancestors engaged them in a great battle at Muscle Shoals, Alabama, forcing the whites to migrate further westward along the Mississippi, the Missouri and the Ohio rivers. Along the way, these Welsh people intermarried with native Indians, eventually joining a tribe now known as the Mandans, who settled along the upper regions of the Missouri.

Sevier went on to relate his meeting with a Frenchman who was captured by the Cherokee and lived among them for some time.

The Frenchman told Sevier he had traded with a tribe of Indians on the Missouri who spoke much of the Welsh dialect. Many of them, particularly the females, were very fair-skinned, and they frequently told the Frenchman they had sprung from a nation of white people.

Explorers Lewis and Clark also told about encounters with strange Indians who exhibited a greater superiority of manner and lifestyle than any they had previously encountered. William Clark, who was in charge of Indian Affairs in the St. Louis area from 1822-1838, declared that the Mandan women were the most beautiful women in the world.

American frontier painter George Catlin lived among the Mandans in the 1830s, and his paintings depicted them with features that were more Welsh than Native American. He wrote that they had a "diversity of complexion, and various colors of hair and eyes," and that some of the women had almost white skin, with hazel, blue or gray eyes.

Like Lewis and Clark, Catlin thought the lives of the Mandans were distinguished from those of other Indians, too. The Mandans lived in permanent homes in villages laid out in squares with streets, surrounded by pickets and trenches or moats. He wrote that they had small boats like the Welsh coracles—round, tub-like vessels made of rawhide stretched over frames of willow. They made blue beads through a process that was a tightly-guarded secret unknown to other Indian tribes. The beads resembled those made through a unique and very old process on the Isle of Lundy off Wales.

Francis Lewis, a signer of the Declaration of Independence, was captured by Indians near Albany, New York, after the fall of Oswego. In his biographies, he says he spoke to his captors in his native Welsh and that they released him. A similar experience was reported by a captured Welsh minister who, having been condemned to death, fell on his knees and prayed to God in the Welsh language. His captors spared him because they understood what he said.

The Mandans were decimated by smallpox in 1837, dwindling from a tribe of 15,000 to a mere 125. The few survivors were absorbed into neighboring tribes. Today, perhaps 300 mixed-blood Mandans are left, and all traces of their original Welsh language have vanished.

But the most compelling physical evidence for Madoc's visit to North America is the stone fortifications that strongly resemble defense systems in ancient Wales. The Welsh depended on natural strategic locations for defense, preferring high, steep mountains or unscalable cliffs for protection. Such requirements fit the stone forts found in Tennessee, Alabama and Georgia.

In 1823, Judge John Haywood wrote in his book, *The Civil and Political History of Tennessee*, that there were five forts in a circle around Chattanooga which had been built by white people living there before the Indian occupation.

"The first was located at the mouth of the Chickamauga Creek outside Chattanooga at a city called Dallas, now covered by the Chickamauga Lake," wrote Irene Parker in *The Welsh Connection*. "A second fort was 20 miles from the mouth of the Chickamauga Creek and a third was at Pumpkinville on the Hiwassee River, now the site of Athens, Tennessee. The most important fort was on the Duck River at Manchester, Tennessee, and was called Old Stone Fort. It comprised 50 acres, triangular in shape, bordered by high bluffs along the forks of the Duck River. The walls of the fort were 20 feet high and 20 feet thick, with a moat connecting the two streams. A fifth fort was at Fort Mountain, Georgia."

It is a sixth fort, at DeSoto Falls near Mentone, that further entwines Alabama in the Madoc legend.

An early Kentucky surveyor noted many similarities between this fort and Dolwyddelan Castle in Gwynedd, including the high, precipitous rock, small entrances, the same arrangement of ditches or moats, and the same method and materials of construction in the walls.

"When Madoc failed to return to his men on the Gulf Coast, evidence indicates they moved inland," Mrs. Parker wrote. "Being seamen, they followed the waterways, up the Alabama and Coosa rivers to the DeSoto Falls area, where they built the first major defensive fort."

The remains of the fort at DeSoto once bore striking similarities to those of Old Stone Fort and Fort Mountain: parallel, moat-encircled stone walls on dangerously high bluffs. Over the centuries, most of the walls at these bastions have fallen and the moats have filled with dirt, although some of the walls of Old Stone Fort are still visible. A modern Indian chief, Joseph "Two Eagles" Stewart, of Maylene, Alabama, says all three forts were built with engineering skills unknown to any Native Americans at that time.

"None of the Cherokees or any other Indians in the Southeast built stone fortifications," says Stewart, who is principal chief of the Echota Cherokee tribe. "They threw up earthen ramparts. These stone fortifications at DeSoto Falls were long, parallel, horseshoe-shaped walls, and if you breached one wall, you came to another one. Indians didn't use that kind of strategy. They fought individually, one-on-one."

The DeSoto Falls fort stood until the mid-1920s, when locals began carrying off its stones to build roads, dams and summer cottages like the one owned by the Rev. Dennis Mays. A retired Methodist minister in Fort Payne, Mays has a cottage on land joining DeSoto State Park and overlooking the falls.

"Part of one of the walls is on our property there," says Mays, who can recall when the wall was still four or five feet high. "I don't know when, where or how it was built, but Madoc seems the most logical answer."

He says the walls were stacked, not mortared, but must have been chiseled out somewhat to make them stay together. All that remains of the walls now are a few stones imbedded in the ground at various points of the horseshoe.

In his *History of Alabama and Incidentally of Georgia and Mississippi From The Earliest Period*, published in 1851, Albert James Pickett described two ancient ditches that curved along the outer side of these walls. The ditches, barely discernible when Pickett visited the site in October, 1850, were nearly parallel, about 30 feet apart over most of their course, but beginning within ten feet of each other on the upper precipice, with their tips joining at the lower end.

The back side of the DeSoto fortification faces a sheer rock bluff that drops into the Little River just below the falls.

About three-quarters of the way up that bluff is a series of five caves. Of natural origin yet apparently enlarged by metal tools, they have passageways between three of their chambers. The caves open immediately onto the precipice, and can be reached from above via Mays's property or from below by a very narrow path clinging to the side of the cliff. Only one man at a time can walk along the precarious path, so that a handful of men stationed near the caves' entrance could destroy multiple attackers simply by hurling them, one by one, to the river 325 feet below.

To reach the caves from Mays's property, one must climb down a dead and hardened pine tree which has lain in the same spot since Mays swam at the falls as a teenager.

"I first remember the caves from my high school days at Valley Head," says Mays, a slim, bearded man who, at 74, still scrambles down the fallen tree with the agility of a monkey. "Anyone would be well-protected if they retreated into that point." Nothing much has ever been found in the caves except for modern campfires and graffiti.

It has been argued that Hernando DeSoto built the fortification and enlarged the caves at the falls bearing his name, but there is no evidence that DeSoto ever saw the falls.

They are not mentioned in any of the three existing journals kept by his men, who surely would have noted such a breathtaking sight.

When early settlers to the region questioned Indians about the origins of the walls and caves, they were told that they were built by white people who wore clothes and sported beards. Never having heard of the Welsh colonists, these settlers probably supposed the Indians to be speaking about DeSoto and his men, who were known to have explored areas of Alabama, Tennessee and Georgia, and so named the falls after the Spaniard.

Perhaps DeSoto had heard of Madoc, though, because other Spanish conquistadors carried a map, extant in Seville today, that bears the word "Madoc," with an arrow pointing to the mouth of the Mobile River.

Despite this mountain of circumstantial evidence, nothing on either side of the Atlantic offers irrefutable proof of the Prince Madoc legend. Too many suppositions and leaps of faith must be made for major historians to take it seriously. Yet, historians and archaeologists alike are beginning to recognize that many conquered people have been denied a history of their own by conquerors who destroyed existing records and re-wrote history to suit themselves.

The legend of Prince Madoc is still an intriguing story that has special meaning for Alabamians and those concerned with her history, who are left to draw their own conclusions.

The Indian Who Caused An Earthquake

Legends about Alabama Indians are as numerous as kudzu vines along the state's roadways. Maidens have dashed themselves on rocky canyon bottoms, lovers from opposing tribes have swum through turbulent waters to meet, and white men have drowned because of an Indian chief's curse on the Black Warrior River.

One legend stands taller than all the rest, however. It is the story of the Indian who was so powerful that the angry stomp of his foot caused the earth to shake, day to turn to night, and rivers to flow backwards.

Tecumseh was the name of this mighty red man. A statesman as well as a warrior, he was chief of the Shawnee Indians, an Algonquin tribe that had migrated from the east to Ohio River country. His campaign to unite the Indians of North America into one group to fight the white men brought him to Alabama. It was here that he made his famous prediction of a great sign from the heavens that would show the Great Spirit's approval of his plan.

Tecumseh was born in 1768, when all of what is now Ohio belonged to the Shawnees and other Indian tribes. Over the years, the Indians of the eastern section of the United States were slowly pushed further and further west beyond the Ohio River by white settlers.

These Indians fought many battles to save their native lands. But the settlers were followed by armies of soldiers, prompting an all-out war between the Indians and the white men in 1791. At first, the battles went well for the Indians, and at one time, they thought they were winning the war.

Tecumseh led many fierce attacks on the white frontier settlements. But he never attacked women and children, and refused to torture prisoners, even though torture was an accepted Indian practice. On one raid in 1792, when some of his warriors mutilated a prisoner, he became so enraged he cursed the guilty braves and ostracized them from the tribe.

But the harder Tecumseh and his fellow Indians fought, the more white soldiers came. Soon, the Indians were outnumbered by the soldiers, who marched where they pleased, burning Indian villages and corn fields, and killing all Indians in their path.

In the winter of 1794, the war officially ended, and Tecumseh hid deep in the forests of Ohio with 100 Shawnee families. They almost starved to death before a messenger came in the spring with word that the whites were offering peace. They wanted Chief Tecumseh to sign a treaty, but he refused. He had seen several treaties broken as whites gobbled up more Indian land. He had no faith in the white man's word.

Several months later, another chief rode into

Tecumseh's village and told him a new treaty had been signed, and the land east of the Ohio River belonged to the white man. He said the whites agreed to let the Indians keep lands farther west, known as Indiana Territory. The white man would build a fort there and send a white governor, but the land would belong to the Indians forever.

So Tecumseh took his people westward, but as for himself, he signed no treaty. He waited to see whether the white men would keep their promise. As he feared, white settlers poured into Indiana Territory despite the treaty. It soon became clear that the white man was reneging on yet another promise. Tecumseh was grieved, because he was losing the land his people had hunted and grew crops on for generations. Yet the whites were so numerous, he did not see how one or two tribes of Indians, with their primitive tomahawks, and their bows and arrows, could fight the endless stream of white soldiers with their powerful muskets.

A dream began to form in the mind and heart of Chief Tecumseh. If every tribe in North America would band together to fight the whites, he reasoned, the Indians would be strong enough to drive the white man out of their land. Evidence of Indian strength in unity was already apparent in the Iroquois Confederacy in New York state. The solidarity of the Iroquois, the Mohawk, Onondaga, Cayuga, Oneida and Seneca had maintained the balance of power between former French owners of Canada and the British colonies for a century.

He also knew of the Creek Confederacy in the Deep South, representing the largest number of unified Indians on the continent. Dominating the Southeast, this confederacy had succeeded in preventing British and Spanish intrusion of their lands for years. Imagine what a confederacy of all Indian tribes could do to repel the white man, Tecumseh thought.

The mighty chief devoted his life to his plan for one

great Indian nation. He traveled throughout the continent, explaining his plan and drumming up support. One version of the Tecumseh legend says that the chief told all the Indians they would receive a sign from Moneta, their supreme god, indicating approval of their enterprise. Then they were to march to Detroit, where Tecumseh's Indian Confederation was headquartered. He suggested that their sheer numbers might cause the whites to back down without a fight.

Riding into the South with his men, Tecumseh held councils with the Cherokees, the Creeks, the Choctaws, Chickasaws and the Seminoles. Like the Iroquois in the East and the Sioux in the West, these tribes agreed to join his cause. According to the most popular version of the Tecumseh legend, it was the refusal of an Alabama Indian that caused the Shawnee chief to predict a terrible sign from the heavens.

Big Warrior, chief of the Alabama Creeks, lived in Tuckabatchee on the Tallapoosa River. He disagreed with Tecumseh's plan. Tecumseh was enraged, and issued a dire warning.

"When I get home, I will stomp my foot on the ground, and the earth will shake," he told Big Warrior. "When this happens, rivers will flow backward, the sun will hide its face, and your village will be destroyed."

A few months later, in the middle of the night on December 16, 1811, a deep rumble began beneath the earth. Indians as far north as the Huron in Canada, as far west as the powerful Sioux nation, and into the Deep South heard and felt the tremors. As Tecumseh had predicted, the mighty Mississippi turned and flowed north for a while, and clouds of dust boiled up to hide the sun.

Settlers in the frontier villages of Kentucky, Ohio, Tennessee and Indiana watched in horror as log cabins and forests alike fell like so many piles of sticks. Huge fissures opened up in the earth, rivers changed their courses, and lakes appeared where sections of land dropped many feet.

At the epicenter of the quake, 60 miles below the mouth of the Ohio River, on the Mississippi, the village of New Madrid disappeared. And in Alabama, the Creek village of Tuckabatchee collapsed. Only the hut where Tecumseh had stayed was left standing.

The quake lasted off and on for two days. It was followed by two more in January, 1812. Then a fourth, hour-long quake on February 13, 1812, caused as much damage as the first three combined. Few Indians remained unconvinced of Tecumseh's great power. Hundreds of warriors from all over the continent headed for Detroit and the Confederation.

But the sign came too late to be of much help to the Indian cause. White troops had already defeated The Prophet, Tecumseh's brother and spokesman, and the Southern tribes were afraid to fight. Then in June of 1812, England and the colonies went to war. Tecumseh, accepting the promise of the British to return the Indians' lands, helped them win several battles with the Americans. The Americans won their war against England, causing more bitterness toward the Indians because of their alliance with the British.

Tecumseh died in 1812, several miles north of Lake Erie, in a battle between the British and the Americans. His warriors buried his body in a secret grave near the battlefield. By the following year, his Confederation had crumbled. But neither his death nor the eventual Indian defeat by the United States could wipe out the legend of the noble Tecumseh, who caused the first earthquake in the history of Alabama's Black Belt by the mere stomping of his foot.

The Death Of Augustus Hatcher Jackson

In the New Cahaba Cemetery near Selma, Alabama, under a white marble slab in a back corner, lie the dust and bones of a prominent Selma attorney who fought nobly for his homeland in the War Between the States. Augustus Hatcher Jackson was not a victim of Yankee bullets, however. Nor did he die of dysentery, the scourge of the Confederate army. Rather, his end was so gruesome, it could have come from a horror story by Edgar Allen Poe.

Augustus Hatcher Jackson was the son of Georgians who had moved to Alabama in the early part of the 19th century. Born December 29, 1829, he graduated with honors from South Carolina College (now the University of South Carolina) in 1852. Coming back to Alabama, he married Jane Elizabeth Gill and practiced law with the firm of Lapsley, Harralson and

Jackson in downtown Selma.

According to Anna Gayle Fry's *Memories of Old Cahaba*, the Jacksons lived on a large plantation just outside Cahaba. The book describes a house situated at the end of a three-mile, rail-bordered lane. The lane was shaded occasionally by peach trees. Originally known as the Muckel place, the house stood in the midst of a grove of large, majestic beech trees.

Apparently, A.H. stayed in town part of the time, however, Cahaba being ten miles and several hours away by horse-drawn carriage. A letter dated June 9, 1860, was posted from Selma to his wife at her family home in nearby Beloit.

In that same letter, Jackson mentions that he has taken ill. His description of his symptoms indicates a prelude to the war-time ailment that indirectly led to his untimely demise.

A good man with a strong sense of right and wrong, Jackson became swept up in the Southern cause and decided to join the Confederate army.

"You don't have to go," his wife, whom he called Jennie, pleaded when he announced his intentions. "It's not your place. I'm so afraid you'll be killed and I'll never see you again."

Probably thinking of the many husbands, sons, fathers and brothers who died in battle, Jennie had no way of knowing that fate had a far more hideous end in store for her husband. Could either of them have seen into the future, had they known of the desperate, final struggle Jackson would undergo, he most surely would not have enlisted. But they did not know, and off he went with his brother to join their fellow Southerners at war.

A.H. enlisted for a year, probably at Cahaba or Selma, and became a private in Company A, 59th Alabama Infantry.

Jennie was unhappy with A.H. for being away. She missed her husband very much, and wanted him home with her, their small twin daughters, Nannie and Lizzie, and an infant son, Augustus Hatcher Jackson Jr., who was born March 26, 1861. Either Jackson came home on furlough, or Jennie visited him at a Confederate camp during the War, because a third daughter, Margaret Loureese, was born in September 1862. That was more than a year after his enlistment, and only two months before the horrifying death of A.H.

Jackson's letters to Jennie sound quite flowery to the modern ear, but they convey the tender emotions of a loving heart. They also paint a touching portrait of a man who was far from home, living in deplorable conditions, who desperately missed his wife and family.

In addition to declaring his undying devotion to his wife, Jackson's letters expressed confidence that Lincoln would soon make peace. If not, he wrote, the Confederate Army would take possession of Washington.

"Kiss the little children for me, so when I get back home I can give their mother all my kisses and so I can receive hers," he affectionately instructed her in one letter.

In another, Jackson described the wretched conditions his regiment had to contend with, conditions that caused about as many deaths during the war as did the actual fighting.

"We are compelled to make sacrifices sometimes," he wrote from Manassa. "You I know have reasons not to be pleased, but what would you think if you could get no water to drink but some muddy in a creek where 15 thousand men wash themselves and (their) clothes in and in which there are dead men laying, but such is my case now and has been for more than awhile."

He said the water was so muddy he could not see the bottom of a cup through it, but he was compelled to drink it because it was the only water available. Small wonder, then, that Jackson came down with dysentery while he and his brother, who served in the same regiment, were just outside Knoxville, Tennessee.

His brother left him in the care of a family there and went to seek medical help. Unfortunately, the family turned out to be abolitionists, who were not uncommon in that portion of the state. Eastern Tennessee was known to have distinct Union leanings, and several counties in the area seceded from Tennessee during the war.

Jackson was not dying as fast as the family would have preferred, though. Perhaps he was even getting better.

"The only good Confederate soldier is a dead one," they reasoned, and proceeded to take matters into their own hands.

Administering what they thought was a fatal dose of a drug or poison to the trusting Jackson, they wasted no time in burying him in a lonely meadow.

A few days later, Jackson's brother returned to find A.H. missing from the bed on which he had been lying. Half crazed with fear, and perhaps suspecting the worst, the brother questioned the host family at length about Jackson's fate.

"Where is he? What have you done with him?" he asked, desperation in his voice.

He had brought a doctor back with him, in the futile attempt to save his brother's life. The doctor apparently knew of the family's abolitionist approbations, and became suspicious.

Finally, the pair wrung a confession from the clan.

With the disbelief that naturally follows such a shock, the brother and the doctor rushed to Jackson's grave site.

Frantically they dug, until they uncovered a rough pine box. They tore at the boards, which yielded reluctantly to the onslaught, as if seeking to conceal as long as possible the anguished truth.

A ghastly sight met their eyes when they pulled open the lid, a sight that forced them to recoil in revulsion and terror.

Jackson was dead, but it was obvious that he had not died peacefully.

His body was crouched in a corner, his legs contorted into a fetal position and his hands drawn up in front of his face.

Slivers of wood under his broken fingernails and scratch marks on the inside of the coffin lid bore mute testimony to his last few moments of life.

How long Jackson had lain unconscious in the cold Tennessee soil was something they could not ascertain. One thing was certain, though. He had awakened from a drug-induced coma and, in a frenzied panic, had tried to claw his way out of his dark prison.

Wiping beads of sweat from his brow, Jackson's brother gently removed the ring and gold pocket watch from the body. He and the doctor closed the coffin, and, amid the stony silence of the abolitionist family, supervised its removal to the railroad station.

What happened to the Tennessee family is anyone's guess, but the body of Augustus Hatcher Jackson was returned to Selma, where he was reburied in a family plot in the New Cahaba Cemetery.

The jewelry A.H. was wearing when he died has been passed down in the family, the ring to the oldest daughter and the watch to the oldest son. John Hatcher Jackson III, of Atlanta, Georgia, is the current owner of his great-great-grandfather's watch.

Jennie remarried after Jackson's death. She died in 1886, at the age of 48, without knowing the truth about her husband's premature burial. The story was not repeated to Jennie or to any other women in the family. None except a small circle of men knew that Augustus Hatcher Jackson actually died in the most horrible manner imaginable: He was buried alive.

*Early railroad tunnels across America
were carved by the hands of steel-driving men
such as the famous John Henry.*

The Day
John Henry Died

The legend of a steel-driving contest between John Henry and the powerful steam drill is a familiar one in American folklore.

More than half a dozen states claim the contest took place within their boundaries, including West Virginia, the most popular site.

But there are some older folks around Leeds, Alabama, who will swear on a stack of Bibles that it actually happened near that Jefferson County town.

John Henry was a large and lively railroad construction worker, possibly an ex-slave. The night he was born, the whole state of Virginia shook like it had been hit by an earthquake.

Some say he weighed 44 pounds at birth, and loved to hammer things even as a baby. By the time he was ten, he could hammer down fence posts as well as any man, and by the age of 18, he was as strong as a locomotive.

Standing over six feet tall, the adult John Henry

was 250 pounds of rippling muscle, which he developed by swinging a nine-pound hammer from sunup to sundown every day. Working for the C&O Railroad, he drove steel into the solid rock that would be blasted out for the Big Bend Tunnel, eight miles east of Hinton, West Virginia.

His partner, Little Bill, would hold a steel spike, called a driver or drill, while John Henry hammered. Between blows, Little Bill would turn John Henry's drill, then he would pull it out when the hole was done. When there were enough holes, the demolition men would fill them with nitroglycerine and blow large gaps for the tunnel.

One of the longest railroad tunnels in America, the Big Bend plowed through one and a quarter miles of West Virginia mountains. Back in 1870, when it was started, a lot of manpower was required to build a tunnel of any kind. So when some Yankees showed up one day with a new-fangled contraption known as a steam drill, claiming it could do the work of three or four men, the construction boss's ears certainly did perk up.

Most folklorists will tell you that the contest between John Henry and the steam drill took place in the Big Bend Tunnel, if it ever took place at all. But one version of the legend says that after making a name for himself on the Big Bend, John Henry swung his hammer on various railroad jobs in several states.

Eventually, he drifted down to the Columbus & Western Railroad, which later became part of the Central of Georgia system, and went to work in the Oak Mountain tunnel on the Columbus-to-Birmingham line of the C&W.

It was here, in the 1,198-foot tunnel about two or three miles south of Leeds, that John Henry challenged the steam drill to a duel. Although he drove a 14-foot hole compared to the drill's nine, he keeled over and died immediately afterward. To this day, his drill sticks out of the hole he was drilling, and old folks around Leeds and nearby Dunnavant will warn you not to disturb it. If you do, you might invoke the spirit of John Henry, who will come out and cast a spell on you.

Today, the Oak Mountain tunnel is part of the Norfolk Southern railroad system, and freight trains still pass through it regularly. It is doubtful that any of the engineers ever notice the ancient bit of metal jutting out of the tunnel wall near the Leeds entrance. Despite the fame of John Henry, few would realize it is the remains of the last steel that the legendary railroad man ever drove.

The body of notorious Railroad Bill
on display in South Alabama.

Railroad Bill: Shape-Shifting Train Robber

Railroad Bill mighty bad man,
Shoot dem lights out de brakeman's han.'
Was lookin' for Railroad Bill.

During the mid 1890s, every lawman in south Alabama was looking for Railroad Bill. A notorious black train robber who also burglarized homes, stole from people and stores, and killed a popular Escambia County sheriff, Bill proved as elusive as the dreams of a Black Belt farmer. How do you catch a man who can change himself into an animal and can only be felled by a silver bullet?

For all the legends surrounding Bill, his background is sketchy. According to one account, Bill, alias Morris Slater, was born in South Carolina during the 1850s, which would put him somewhere between 36 and 45 when he started his life of crime. He came to the Parker Springs community outside Brewton as a young man, tending sheep and hogs for a while, then eking out a living making turpentine in the piney woods of south Alabama and northern Florida. Later, those same woods would shelter and protect Bill when he ran afoul of the law.

He claimed to have spent a few years with a circus, which would explain the various hand tricks he often performed for street audiences. He could swallow a whole egg and spit it back up without breaking the shell and could walk and run on his hands. Bill often picked up a few coins by passing his hat among his audiences after finishing one of his acts.

A newspaper account at Bill's death said he was working at a turpentine camp near Bluff Springs, Florida, about five miles below Flomaton, when his criminal career began. After repeatedly refusing to buy a license for the Winchester rife he always carried, he got into a battle with Deputy Sheriff Allen Brewton and a group of citizens who were trying to enforce Florida's gun law. In the ensuing confrontation, a bullet from Bill's gun nipped an ear of one of the good citizens. It was about this time that Bill decided Baldwin County, Alabama, might be a safer place to live, after all.

Bill must have wearied of the meager living his tricks and trades afforded, because he took to robbing trains. He would hop onto a car loaded with goods, toss out what he wanted between stations, then hop off. He would pick up the loot at his leisure, usually selling it on the underground market.

Particularly fond of the L&N line between Brewton and Mobile, he frequently distributed the food he stole to hungry black families who lived along that route. In return, they would let him sleep in front of their fires and kept him informed when the law got too close. Some even kept him supplied with ammunition.

Making the isolated woods and swamps his headquarters, Bill became bolder and more frequent with his raids on the northern-owned railroads. He would routinely rob boxcars, depots and stores, taking what he needed and terrorizing anyone in his way.

Some newspaper accounts also told of him breaking into homes and stealing clothing, or waylaying travelers.

Bill had several close calls with the various authorities who were after him. In August, 1894, the conductor and crew of an L&N train imprisoned him in a boxcar, but Bill managed to shoot his way out. In March of 1895, he was involved in another gun battle near Mobile, and in a similar incident, he killed one of the dogs that had tracked him to the swamps. In fact, he shot his way out of so many encounters that many people were convinced he could catch the bullets in his hands and could only be killed by a silver one.

When Bill was not dodging bullets, he simply outwitted the law. On one occasion, Escambia County Sheriff Ed McMillan and his officers took a train to a lonesome place where they thought the desperado was hiding. But Bill was actually in the boxcar behind them all the time, and when they got off the train to look for him, he just stayed on board and collected canned goods that he gave away all over Escambia County that night.

Every time he escaped the law or one of the railroad detectives, another verse would be added to one of the many folk songs about his exploits. Oddly enough, none of the songs mentioned his Robin Hood characteristics, and one even depicts him as stealing from the poor. "Railroad Bill, got so bad/ Stole all the chickens the poor farmers had," that version notes.

Perhaps this dichotomy of character added an element of fear among the folks who helped him elude the authorities. Or perhaps the hoodoo and magic he was said to have learned in the dark piney woods simply worked to his advantage among the superstitious folk of his day. Whatever the reason, Bill picked up a reputation as a shape-changer who could always escape a tight situation by shifting his form into that of a rabbit, sheep, fox, dog, bear, or any other animal he chose. He was also credited with the ability to make himself invisible.

One woman swears she saw Bill coming down the railroad track one day and turn himself into a sheep before he got to her.

Another time, Sheriff McMillan and his deputies were running through the woods after Bill. As they raced through a clearing, they saw a black sheep just standing there, watching them. They did not realize until long afterwards that the clearing was a mighty strange place for a sheep to be.

During another hunt, the sheriff followed Bill's tracks through the swamp, but when he came to a little clearing, the tracks stopped. The sheriff decided Bill must be hiding under some low bushes, and began looking around. Pretty soon he startled a little red fox that lit out through the woods. The sheriff let go with both barrels of his shotgun, but he missed.

After the second shot, the little red fox turned around and laughed at him. The sheriff recognized that high, wild and hearty laugh, and realized he had been foiled again. The fox was actually Railroad Bill.

But the time that made the sheriff the maddest was when Bill chased himself to his girlfriend's house. McMillan heard Bill had been courting a good-looking woman over by Piney Grove. So he got some blood-hounds from a man in Mississippi and let them sniff one of the old hats Bill had dropped during one of his escapes. Sure enough, the dogs picked up Bill's scent on a trail that led straight for Piney Grove.

In a little while, the sheriff wondered out loud about the number of dogs he had rented.

"Did we get three dogs or four from Bob Gant?" he asked. Nobody could remember, but they did notice there were four dogs on the trail, including a black bloodhound.

When they came to the cabin of Bill's girlfriend, she was standing on the front porch.

"Have you seen Bill?" the sheriff asked her.

"No, I haven't, for sure," she replied.

The dogs seemed to want to go on, so the sheriff and his men followed them. Soon enough, the sheriff noticed there were but three bloodhounds on the trail. The black one was gone.

Of course, the sheriff did not find Bill on that trip, and when he took the dogs back to their owner, he discovered he had rented only three. Apparently, the sheriff never knew that the black hound was really Bill, who had chased himself all the way to his girlfriend's house and had stayed behind to do some courting when the posse left.

Then on April 6, 1895, an attempt to capture Bill near Hurricane Bayou in Baldwin County resulted in the death of Deputy Sheriff J.H. Stewart. Soon, posters appeared on the walls of small-town depots in south Alabama, describing him as "the notorious Bay Minette desperado," and offering a $500 reward for his capture, dead or alive. He was described in a notice at Union Depot in Mobile as 5'6", weighing about 150 pounds, with "uncommonly high cheek bones and a broad face." Yet another description of Bill, from a newspaper account of a man's encounter with him, described Bill as "about five feet ten inches in height, weight about 175 pounds, and 38-40 years of age."

Bill's legendary escapes were enough to endure, but when the outlaw killed a fellow lawman, Sheriff McMillan became more determined than ever to capture the elusive bandit. Bill got wind of McMillan's vow to bring him in. Sitting in a tumbledown shack with some friends, he swore no man could capture him because of his shape-changing abilities.

"I likes Ed McMillan," Bill told his companions. "I

worked in his turpentine still and he's a fine man. He mustn't come after me, or I'll have to use my gun. I'm gonna write him a letter."

With the stub of a pencil, he wrote the sheriff a rather unusual note on an old piece of paper in big letters. "Don't come, Mr. Ed. I love you," the note read.

McMillan told his brothers about the note. They suggested he might be better off forgetting about Bill, but the sheriff said he was sworn to uphold the law, so he had to go after him.

On July 3, 1895, McMillan learned that Bill was holed up near Bluff Springs, and he immediately organized a small posse to go after him. They traced him to Bluff Springs, and began closing in on some shanties he was known to frequent. About 9 p.m. the posse was coming up the railroad through a dense oak grove when a cry of "Halt!" greeted them. From behind a tree a rifle shot erupted. McMillan turned in the direction of the tree, gun in hand, and a second shot caught him near the heart.

Newspaper accounts differed as to what happened next. One article said the confrontation ended with McMillan taking the bullet. Another, however, recorded that a Negro man came from behind the tree, and one of the posse, a Dr. O'Bannon, fired squarely at him, bringing him down. Confident that Railroad Bill was "shot to pieces," as the article put it, posse members nevertheless refused to go to him, for fear he was only wounded and might rise up to kill one of them. Besides, McMillan commanded their attention.

"Are you hurt bad?" one of the posse asked.

"Yes, I'm killed," McMillan replied. A few hours later, the sheriff died.

At daybreak, a heavy rain set in over Brewton. Word soon spread about the previous night's events, and Independence Day festivities were forgotten as the town mourned its popular sheriff. Everyone assumed the man who had stepped from behind the tree to kill Sheriff McMillan was Railroad Bill, even though no one had gone close enough to verify his identity or to check his wounds. When Railroad Bill was sighted again, however, folks knew O'Bannon had not killed him after all. The price on Bill's head was increased to more than $1,200. The L&N sweetened the bait with an offer of a lifetime pass to anyone who brought down the outlaw.

For two more years Bill remained on the loose, with law enforcement agencies, railroad detectives and private investigators on his trail. Several times he would be cornered, but would shoot his way out. But on March 7, 1897, the outlaw's reign of terror ended in a hail of bullets at a little store on the outskirts of Atmore.

A posse headed by Constable Leonard McGowin had given up a day-long search and was gathered at Tidmore and Ward's general merchandise store, preparing to disband for the night. Imagine their surprise when Bill walked in, and without his trusty Winchester in hand.

Either he was relying upon the belief that people thought him hidden deep in the swamps, or his bravado was such that he thought he could walk into that store and, by his very presence, make everyone else run out. Such recklessness cost him his life.

McGowin spied him, raised his own rifle to his shoulder, and shot him. When the outlaw fell to the floor, bullets started flying from every direction as other members of the posse tried to get a piece of the action. This time, Bill was dead before he had time to work his hoodoo and change shapes.

Even with the right side of his face blown away, and his right hand mangled, people familiar with Bill were able to identify the body. In the post-mortem, a Dr. McLendon said he found about 15 different gunshot wounds, but the first shot fired by McGowin had proven fatal. Nevertheless, a dispute arose between

McGowin and the store's owner over who should get the reward, but the two eventually decided to divide it between them.

A special train took the body from Atmore to Brewton, where it was embalmed and photographed, then put on display. It drew a crowd of at least 3,000 people, who came from all directions in ox carts, on mule back or on foot, to see the remains of the infamous outlaw.

An old black woman made a grand speech to the crowds, warning all the other men not to follow the steps that Bill had taken. Declaring how his broken body was ample evidence that a life of crime could only lead to a bad end, she also pointed out that an ordinary lead bullet would kill a desperado as easily as a silver one.

The legend existed for years that Ed Leigh McMillan, who was about seven when his father died, picked a handful of bitterweeds and put them in Bill's mouth while his body was displayed in Brewton. Not only did McMillan dispute this legend in his personal correspondence in 1977, but, as Kathryn Tucker Windham pointed out in her book, *Alabama: One Big Front Porch*, bitterweeds do not bloom in March.

The body was finally placed in a metallic casket and shipped to Montgomery, where it was again put on exhibition. From the capital city, it was exhibited at south Alabama depots all the way from Greenville to Mobile, with folks lining up and paying from $.25 to $.50 to see it. Many had their photographs made with the late Railroad Bill, and one still exists of Constable McGowin standing next to the bare-footed corpse.

After killing and robbing his way into infamy, Bill reportedly was put to rest in an unmarked grave. But for years many blacks throughout south Alabama refused to believe he was dead. More than 30 years after the outlaw's death, when the government would send commodities to hungry folks to keep them from starving during the Great Depression, some of them swore the food came from Railroad Bill.

Even today, many will swear that Railroad Bill is still roaming around Bay Minette, Flomaton and Bluff Springs. Sometimes he's a sheep, sometimes he's a dog, sometimes he's a hog or a rabbit, but always he's laughing.

A woman of haunting eyes:
The young and beautiful Hazel Farris.

Hazel Farris: A Well-Preserved Woman

Step right up, ladies and gentlemen. See Hazel the Mummy. She's 55 years old and weighs only 33 pounds. Gaze upon her face. Touch her leathery skin.

Examine her long, flowing hair. She's real, she's genuine. Don't miss the only human mummy in the world today outside of museums.

When Hazel Farris asked her husband for a new hat, she had no idea that such a simple request, and his steadfast refusal, would lead to a life of infamy. First, she became a criminal with a price on her head, then she became Alabama's most celebrated mummy.

Young, beautiful and admired in her community near Louisville, Kentucky, Hazel had a dark side to her personality. A headstrong woman, she argued with her husband about the hat. No one knows why he objected to the purchase. Maybe the hat was more than they could afford. Maybe Hazel already had a closet full of hats. Whatever his reasons, he must have seemed unreasonable to Hazel. Words passed between them, gunfire rang out, and her husband fell dead on the floor.

Three passing policemen heard the shots and ran into the Farris house to investigate. Pistol-packing Hazel shot them, too.

A deputy sheriff, already summoned, arrived on the scene. Slowly, he entered through the back door, took the crazed woman by surprise and attempted to overpower her. In the ensuing struggle, his revolver went off, taking with it the ring finger from Hazel's right hand. As he stood up, Hazel fired a fifth bullet, and another body was added to the pile.

The sound of gunfire attracted a crowd, and in the excitement, Hazel managed to escape. A $500 reward was posted for her capture, and she fled the state, settling in her hometown of Bessemer, Alabama. She became a lonely fugitive who, according to local wags, earned her living on her back. She fell in love, and made the fatal mistake of trusting her lover with information about her past. He betrayed her to the police, and on December 20, 1906, at the age of 25, Hazel apparently took poison rather than go to jail.

Her body was taken to a local furniture store, which was not unusual for that time. Furniture stores frequently sold caskets back then, and peddled mortuary services on the side.

"They usually would trim the boxes out, and when people came in to buy one, they would sell them the funeral services, too," says Dr. William Counce, an instructor in the Funeral Service Education Department at Jefferson State Community College in Birmingham, Alabama. "That's where a lot of funeral homes started, in furniture stores and livery stables."

Time passed, and Hazel began to mummify. Some

local sages figured her preservation was due to a mixture of the whiskey she was so fond of, her passion, and the arsenic they think she used to end her life. Others say it was the repeated injections of embalming fluid.

"I remember hearing stories about how the original undertaker kept filling Hazel with formaldehyde over the next several months, trying to preserve her while waiting for someone to claim her," says Catherine Kean, a volunteer at the Bessemer Hall of History.

Louise Tommie, another Hall of History volunteer, questions whether Hazel was embalmed at all. "Some of the fascination with Hazel is the mystery surrounding the circumstances of her death and subsequent preservation," says Mrs. Tommie. She has spoken with several older Bessemer residents who remembered Hazel, including the daughter of the furniture-store-cum-mortuary owner, and none could remember embalming being involved.

However, Alabama's embalming laws are among the oldest in the nation, according to Dr. Counce. The Board of Examiners of Embalmers was created by the State Assembly in December, 1894, and Dr. Counce does not see how anyone could have gotten around the laws in 1906.

Embalming fluid frequently was arsenic-based in the early 1900s.

"Arsenic was much more effective than formaldehyde," Dr. Counce says. "People embalmed with arsenic tend to dehydrate, which is different than a specified mummification process like the ancient Egyptians used. There were recipes floating around where funeral directors could make the fluid themselves. In fact, in 1906, the embalming fluid market probably was not commercially accessible around here like it is today, so it might have been just as easy to make it themselves. That might make it a very astringent arsenic base."

Whether or not Hazel was embalmed remains part of her mystique, but we know for sure that she did not deteriorate like most bodies do. She continued to dehydrate, however, leaving deep folds of tough, leathery skin. Soon, she looked more like an old crone of 100 than the beautiful 25-year-old redhead she had been at death. Word spread about this mysterious mummy, and the curious came in droves to see it. The store owner/mortician charged $.10 per view. Still, no one claimed her.

Later, she was transferred to another furniture store in Tuscaloosa, according to Mrs. Tommie. About a year after Hazel's death, a carny who had heard of Hazel bought her mummified remains for $25.

"Uncle Olanda first brought her to Nashville and put her in my grandmother's garage," says Luther Brooks, a grand-nephew of O.C. Brooks, the man who purchased Hazel. "He left her there while he went to Louisville to try and find her relatives. He did find several people who knew her, but no one who wanted her body."

For many years, O.C. Brooks made a comfortable living exhibiting Hazel "for scientific purposes," according to his carnival flyers. "Now in this city, Hazel Farris in dehydration," his flyers proclaimed. "Moral exhibit for benefit of science." He offered a $500 reward to anyone who could prove she was a fake.

O.C. Brooks claimed it was the only genuine human mummy in the world except for a few Egyptian subjects in some of the larger museums. (Either the mummies of Guanajuato, Mexico, had not been discovered at that time, or Brooks was unaware of them.)

"It is a natural mummy and a better subject than any of the Egyptian class, which have to be kept in airtight glass cases," his flyers stated. "Hazel is exhibited in the open air so that all may examine the beautiful suit of long, flowing hair."

It was her hair that further contributed to Hazel's

mystique. Some stories say that her hair and nails continued to grow for 35 years, although why they suddenly stopped fosters yet another mystery. When you repeat this story today, people nod their heads and say that hair and nails continue to grow for a period of time on all corpses. But Jack Parker, deputy coroner for Jefferson County, says it is not so.

"In reality, the body starts dehydrating and decomposing, and the skin shrinks, making the hair and nails appear longer," Parker says.

Luther Brooks still believes the legend, however. "My Granny Brooks, who wouldn't tell a lie, said she cut Hazel's hair and fingernails regularly during the five years she was in her west Nashville garage," Brooks says.

To prevent anyone from stealing Hazel, his uncle apparently slept on top of the old pine box that housed her. That's where the old carny's body was found April 1, 1950, in the barn where he had lived in Coushatta, Louisiana. Luther Brooks, who was 13 years old at the time, remembers traveling to Louisiana with his father to claim his uncle's remains.

"Nobody in the family would go except my dad," Luther explains. "We went down and he had Uncle Olanda buried. People gave us all of my uncle's stuff, including Hazel, so we took her home with us."

Within a couple of years, Luther's father had left his family, placing Hazel in Luther's possession. Luther was in the ninth grade when he started showing Hazel at school carnivals, a practice he continued through high school.

"When I finished high school in 1958, I had a small carnival myself, with nine amusements and Hazel," he says.

A few years ago, his wife discovered among his uncle's possessions a notebook that detailed Hazel's appearances during the Great Depression. According to those records, O.C. Brooks made $150 to $200 a week showing Hazel, a hefty sum for that economic period. One wonders how many new hats that would have bought.

Luther Brooks sold his small carnival in 1965, and put Hazel in semi-retirement at his Nashville-area home. Over the next few years, mortuary science students from nearby Vanderbilt University came by each year and examined Hazel. From the amount of folded skin, they determined she must have weighed about 165 pounds the day she died.

In 1974, the Bessemer Hall of History contracted with Brooks to display her locally. By then 93 years old, Hazel was in remarkable condition for a woman her age. Thousands of people paid $.50 each during her first re-appearance in October 1974, in an old, otherwise empty building in downtown Bessemer. A skylight illuminated her casket as she lay in the middle of a large room, with people walking all around her.

Three more times over the next seven years, Hazel received visitors for about three weeks around Halloween at the Hall of History's original location in the basement of the city's library, 1830 Fourth Avenue North. The museum moved to the old Bessemer train depot during the mid-1980s.

She also appeared at the Alabama State Fair for a week and at the University of Alabama's Ferguson Student Center for another week in October 1975, according to that month's edition of *The Hush Puppy*, the newsletter of the West Jefferson County Historical Society.

Over the years, Hazel became a little worse for the wear.

She lost two gold teeth in 1959, when the tent fell on a Nashville carnival and a group of women accidentally turned her casket over and dumped Hazel into the sawdust, according to Luther Brooks. The little finger on her left hand was eaten by rats back when his uncle had her.

"The rats died in the casket, though," Brooks adds.

Louise Tommie, the unofficial "Hazel Chairman" for the mummy's Bessemer visits, has a favorite Hazel story that revolves around an imperative cleaning.

"We were hiding her in the basement of the library, because the librarian couldn't stand the thoughts of her being there," Mrs. Tommie recalls. "But Hazel had mold on her. I went to the dry cleaners and asked what I could clean her with. The owner didn't offer to do it, but gave me a big jug of ammonia-smelling fluid."

Hazel was stiff, but she was not very heavy. Mrs. Tommie picked her up, intending to take her to a larger room than where she was kept hidden. About the time she was walking out the door, she spotted the librarian coming down the stairs.

"I had Hazel under one arm like a board, so I just turned her in the middle of the hallway, went back into the room where we were hiding her, and closed the door," she says.

Eventually, Mrs. Tommie did manage to get Hazel laid out on some paper on the floor, and cleaned the mold off her. She was also the woman who usually returned Hazel to Luther Brooks after each showing, with Hazel making the trip in the back of Mrs. Tommie's station wagon.

Exhibition contracts in Hazel's file at the Hall of History indicate that when she was shown there in 1981, the $.50 fee was up to $1 per adult and $.50 per child. All proceeds from these local visits went to the Hall of History, with Luther Brooks receiving a ten percent cut. A newspaper article from the late 1970s indicates Hazel earned about $6,000 for the museum during her first three visits.

"I remember the time in 1981 when she was displayed here," says Ed Kean, husband of Catherine Kean and owner of Kean Advertising Agency in Bessemer. "She was deteriorating by then, and she was beginning to smell. We had to get an undertaker to come in and put a deodorant in the box with her."

Hazel always smelled bad when her casket was kept closed, according to Luther Brooks, who says she looks the same today as she did 20 years ago. "It was a musty odor, and when you opened up the casket and let her air out, you wouldn't know it," Brooks says.

Folks at the Hall of History claim it was mere coincidence that Hazel always appeared around Halloween, and Luther Brooks swears he never used Hazel to scare anyone. She resides today in her box in the recreation room of his Tennessee home.

He did not show her publicly after 1981, until she made a return Halloween appearance at the Bessemer Hall of History in 1994. He has allowed an occasional private peek between showings, however.

"She may have been a bad girl in life, but in death she did a lot of good," Brooks believes.

She lost two gold teeth in 1959, when the tent fell on a Nashville carnival and a group of women accidentally turned her casket over and dumped Hazel into the sawdust.

The Beast Of New Cahaba Cemetery

It was a dark, cold, moonless night, perfect for rabbit hunting. That is what 16-year-old John Rowell and his friend thought as they pulled into the "new" cemetery at Old Cahaba.

Hoping to catch a few rabbits in the car's headlights and pick them off easily with his .22, Rowell was riding on the front fender of a '56 Mercury convertible. His friend turned the car around and parked near a large clump of bushes just inside the gate.

One of several old graveyards in the area, the New Cahaba Cemetery, as it is often called, was established in 1851, when the town of Cahaba (Alabama's first capitol) still thrived.

Overgrown with shrubs, vines and bushes during the 1950s, the new cemetery claims some of Cahaba and Selma's most prominent citizens as permanent residents.

Several hundred people are buried in New Cahaba Cemetery. Most of their wooden markers have been lost to the ravages of time and vandalism. Marble monuments and slabs, marred and crumbling but clearly visible, still delineate 70 of the sites. On a dark night, the tallest of the tombstones become silent sentinels that can turn into monsters at the slightest hint of fear.

Teenage boys are not afraid of old tombstones, however. Nor do they jump at the sound of bullfrogs croaking in the swamps.

But when bushes begin to move and part, well, that is another matter.

"That night, the bushes just started making a big ruffling, moving, shaking sound, like something was in there," John Rowell recalls. "Then we heard this thing holler. It was a high-pitched sound, sort of a cross between a panther and a woman screaming. The boy with me said, 'Man, let's get outta here.' We took off, and that was our introduction to the Wampus Cat."

Rowell is not sure where the term "Wampus Cat" came from, but that is what he and his friends started calling the mysterious night prowler. It became common practice for them to visit the New Cahaba Cemetery in search of the creature.

"We didn't have much to do back then, not a whole lot to get into, and we'd go rabbit huntin' a lot or just ride around at night, talk, one thing and another," says Rowell, describing a slower, calmer time. "This got to be just a phenomenon that was exciting and intriguing to kids, to want to get out and hear something like that."

Before long, they started venturing further and further into the cemetery, listening for that high-pitched scream of terror.

Rowell soon discovered that by imitating the sound, he could call up the unseen beast from its swampy lair.

"We started parking about halfway into the cemetery, because we could see better there, and it always came over the fence at the left back corner, from the direction of the swamps. None of the big pines surrounding the cemetery today were here then, it was all open around the outside. Lots of times, you could hear it as it would come up on the fence, and the fence would make a noise as it vibrated, whang, whang whanggg."

When Rowell would call it, its first reply would be distant and faint, placing the beast about three or four miles away. Every two or three minutes, it would scream again, a little closer and from another direction. It did not take a genius to figure out it was circling the cemetery, or that its circles were getting smaller and smaller.

"We mainly came down here in the winter, during hunting season, but it got to where it didn't matter when we came," Rowell says. "We'd just sit around and talk. Of course, the more we'd talk, the scareder we'd get, and the more things we'd see."

They never actually saw the Wampus Cat.

"We saw its eyes glowing in the dark one night, but we never could get a light on it. It was fast, and we were scared, especially the time it jumped on our car."

That night, Rowell and his friends were sitting in the Mercury. Because it was winter, the car's top was up, and the guys were trying to see how long they could stay before they chickened out and ran. Rowell let out with his wampus cat wail, and they heard the fence twang as the creature entered the cemetery. Closer and closer it came, screaming every three or four minutes. Soon, it was circling the car.

"You could hear it walking in the brush around us, and we just stayed real quiet and listened," Rowell says. "The last time it hollered it was right behind the car, real close. Then we felt the back of the car go down. That got our attention real good. We couldn't stand it any longer, we had to go. We could picture it tearing through that canvas top. I don't know how fast we left, but when we got back up to the street light, about a mile up the road, we stopped and looked at the back of the car. In the frost on the car were two big scrapes, each about eight to 10 inches wide, going right off the back end."

Despite such a close encounter, Rowell continued his nocturnal cemetery visits. Many of the people he brought with him remained crouched on the floorboard of his car throughout their visit, so horrifying was the demon's eerie cry. Others were braver, actually walking into the cemetery with no protection.

They would sit on a grave slab with Rowell, talking around a lantern and waiting for the monster's arrival. Fortunately for the walkers, the Wampus Cat did not come every time it was called.

"I got real brave one night and carried a friend out there, determined to solve the mystery," Rowell says. "We each carried a shotgun, and I said to my friend, 'Listen, we're gonna catch this thing, and find out for sure what it is.'

"My friend kept telling me he wasn't scared of anything, how he was with me all the way, but really, he was more than a little skittish.

" 'You're not gonna back out on me, are you?' I asked him.

" 'No, I'm with you,' he said.

"We hollered for the cat two or three times, and didn't hear anything. Then we heard a rustlin' noise in the canebrake along the right side the cemetery, near the back.

"I said, 'You hear that?'

"He said, 'Yeah, I hear it.'

"I said, 'Something's down in that corner, isn't it?'

"He said, 'Sure is, must be that old cat.'

"I said, 'You ready to go get it?'

"And he said, 'Yeah, yeah, I'm with you.'

"So we got out of the car, and both of us started walking toward the corner where the sound was coming from. I guess we got about 15 feet from it when the canebrake started parting. I never will forget it. Our eyes were getting big, but we couldn't see too much. It was real dark, and we had no lights with us.

"All of a sudden, it broke loose and came right at us. My brave friend wrapped his arms and legs around me, pushing my shotgun up my nose. Two big black things were right on top of us by then. If they had been boogers they would have eaten us up.

"Luckily, we didn't shoot, because we'd have killed somebody's two good mules!"

Another night, Rowell and a friend took some hunting dogs down to the cemetery, again determined to track and capture the elusive Wampus Cat. The group was in an old Dodge station wagon, the kind with a rear window that could be raised and lowered electrically. Rowell called the cat, it answered, and he could hear it circling closer and closer.

"We had those dogs in the back, and the cat went to hollering," Rowell recalls. "It got pretty close, and we pushed the button that lowered the rear window. They were pretty good hunting dogs, supposed to run anything, but as fast as we would throw 'em out the back of the station wagon, they would whimper and jump back in. They wouldn't run it at all. I don't know what that indicated, other than that they were as scared as we were.

"Needless to say, we didn't stay much longer that night."

Between nocturnal visits to the cemetery, Rowell did some daylight investigating. He soon discovered that others were aware of the beast's existence.

"We heard tales from different people, mostly folks living down there, about panthers or cougars and different things happening on the (Alabama) River," Rowell says. "One old man who fished on the river said the creature had run him off many times."

" 'You just can't stay when it gets to hollering,' the

man told me. 'There ain't no way, you'll just have to leave, because it will scare you so bad.'

"And it will. It will absolutely make your hair stand up on your head."

Although Rowell's cemetery excursions continued over a period of 10-to-15 years, they gradually ceased as more pressing matters—marriage, work, children—crowded his adult life.

It has been 15 years since he heard the cat, and a spring 1994 attempt to call it up proved futile.

"I've lost my voice for it," he says, more amused than sad.

"I can't get my voice up that high anymore. Besides, the night I tried, there was too much moonlight. It was always pitch dark when we'd hear it. A wild animal doesn't like a lot of light, if a wild animal is what it was."

"...We heard this thing holler. It was a high-pitched sound, sort of a cross between a panther and a woman screaming."

—John Rowell

Mine shaft searches did not turn up missing youths.

Three Men And A Car Vanish

The Dye-Brasher Mystery

It was one of those rainy March nights so typical of Birmingham, when winter clings to its last vestiges of cool weather. Rain pelted the roofs, causing most folks to burrow under the covers and pray that seasonal tornadoes were not following the path of the rain.

Despite the lateness of the hour, peals of laughter rang from an unpainted cabin on Crooked Creek Road in Sardis, a north Jefferson County mining community near Morris. Whiskey distilled in the surrounding woods was passed around in a five-gallon jug, keeping spirits high and the dampness out. Couples danced to a tune played on a pocket comb covered with tissue paper.

Like many at that party, two young Fultondale brothers, Robert Earl Dye, 23, and Billy Howard Dye, 20, along with their cousin, Dan Brasher, 38, of Morris, had started drinking early in the day. It was Saturday, and nobody in that God-fearing land worked on Sundays, unless it was to stoke the fires under his moonshine still.

In an earlier party that same night, the three relatives had gotten into an argument, although witnesses later swore that it did not really amount to much. They left together, dropping off Robert's wife, Audrey, at her home. Apparently, they also stopped to see Ellen Brasher, Dan's mother. In a newspaper article dated March 12, 1956, Mrs. Brasher, who lived near Morris, reported that the trio left her house around midnight. Still swigging on their whiskey jugs, they headed for the larger party on Crooked Creek Road.

Sometime before dawn, the trio left the second party in Billy's dark green 1947 Ford, license plate 1A-7088. No one knows where they were going, and no one has admitted seeing them since.

The disappearance of the Dye brothers and their cousin on March 4, 1956, is one of the most baffling cases ever recorded by Jefferson County lawmen. Caves and mine shafts have been explored, highways bored and dug up over the years since that fateful night, but no identifiable trace of the men or Billy's car has ever been found.

From the very beginning, everyone suspected foul play. The Dye brothers had been working on the construction of the "new" four-lane U.S. 31, north of Birmingham. One week after their disappearance, they still had not called for their paychecks. Dan Brasher was supposed to begin his own construction job the Monday after the party. The trio reportedly had only $25 among them the night they disappeared.

A relative of the men, the Rev. R.L. Brasher of Gardendale, told police the Dye boys had a reputation of never being away from home overnight without informing their mother.

Almost everyone involved with the case knew that it had to do with the moonshine racket. The rugged hill country around Morris was bootleg territory when the men disappeared, and had been since long before Prohibition days. Whiskey had been stolen from some of the moonshiners, and they were upset about it. A moonshiner who suspected the trio of stealing his whiskey may have been among the guests at the last party the men attended. And Dan Brasher had served jail time for moonshining.

When the boys failed to come home that rainy March night, relatives did not think much about it at first. They knew the men could get rowdy when they drank, and figured they were probably in jail somewhere for drunken driving. The following Wednesday, Curtis Brasher, a first cousin to all three men, and his father searched jails from Morris to Decatur. They contacted the Sheriff's Department on Thursday and reported them missing.

The next day, Brasher and his father tried to visit a Morris moonshiner, but were stopped before they reached his house. The moonshiner's cousin told the Brashers that the bodies had been found and an arrest had been made. The Brashers left, only to discover that the man had lied. In a subsequent visit to Curtis Brasher, the man admitted lying, saying he did not want them to see the 1947 Ford in the moonshiner's barn.

As the search continued, it focused so much attention on the remote section where the men had partied and drank that many moonshiners were unable to operate with their usual freedom.

It also caused some bad blood among them, as they accused each other of responsibility in the case and blamed each other for bringing the law down on all of them. The law began to crack down on the area, and the flow of moonshine slowed to a trickle.

The moonshiners were not the only people upset

with the official investigation. Curtis Brasher was unhappy about it too, but for vastly different reasons. He harbored questions of whether the sheriff's department had deliberately slowed its investigation.

So he started his own. He poked into abandoned mine shafts, crawled through dark caves, and peered down wells all over north Jefferson and Blount counties. He found nothing. He posted a $2,000 reward. It was never claimed.

Soon, Brasher, who eked out a living as a mechanic, was devoting most of his spare time and what little money he had to the case. He became an amateur sleuth, logging thousands of miles tracking down clues all over the state. He wrote letters to public officials on the county, state and national level, including then FBI Director J. Edgar Hoover.

"I can understand killing a man under certain circumstances, but the bodies shouldn't be buried like an animal, just crammed into some hole or put underground like garbage," Brasher once said.

He thought he had hit pay dirt when he and other family members stumbled upon three graves in secluded Layfield Hollow, between Clay and Village Springs in north Jefferson County. But the graves turned out to be where someone had been digging for Indian artifacts.

Brasher kept up his letter-writing campaign, and eventually gained the attention of the state Department of Public Safety. He also drew community support, as evidenced by the petition he gave then-Sheriff Holt Howell. Signed by hundreds of residents, it urged that the investigation be stepped up. Not long afterwards, the sheriff assigned Deputy Tom Ellison to the case.

Curtis Brasher continued to probe, ask questions and follow up leads. His information led him to an old watery shaft called Black Diamond Mine, between Fultondale and Ketona.

Brasher's brother, Jim, fished out a hank of red hair, causing a collective gasp among the Dye-Brasher families. Dan Brasher's hair had been red. A state toxicologist said the red hair belonged to a human, but the original color was a light blond.

The Dye brothers had been dark haired, so that pretty much ruled out any connection with the trio.

Not satisfied with the official report, Brasher rounded up some scuba divers to voluntarily go down into the black, murky hole for a look. They found nothing, but the site preyed on Brasher's mind. He managed to get the shaft pumped partially dry with loaned equipment. There were no bodies there.

Over the years, mines and mine shafts continued to play important roles in the search for the missing men.

The Happy Hollow Mine or "Old Glory," off New Castle Road near Bradford, yielded a tennis shoe the same size worn by one of the missing men, along with glass from a car window.

Investigators thought perhaps the killers had put the missing men in the mine and then dynamited it. A bulldozer uncovered no evidence.

Curtis Brasher picked up a clue once that the bodies might possibly be in some old mining test holes sunk years earlier between Ketona and Pinson. County bulldozers moved in to ferret out the evidence, producing nothing but some metal that could have been from a car similar to Billy Dye's Ford.

In April, 1960, an abandoned mine in north Jefferson County pricked the interest of the authorities.

The mine was once owned by the father of a man who, according to newspaper reports, was subjected to a lie detector test regarding the case. Although investigators would not say whether the man passed the test, they did say that his answers gave them additional hope.

Various bits of information, including evidence that a car had been burned at the mouth of the mine, led officers to open it. When rains and wet ground hampered their efforts, many remembered the rainy night the men disappeared, and took it as a favorable sign. Unfortunately, they were wrong, because the mine yielded nothing.

Every now and then, a new story would trickle down from the hills about somebody claiming knowledge of the case. Deputies checked out every story, which usually ended with a denial by the person to whom the story had been attributed, or with admission that he "talked too much," and did not really know anything.

One of the most bizarre tales came from a man who lived near the last house where the missing men had partied. He said that early on March 4, 1956, some men carried tub after tub of water from his outdoor faucet into that house, which had no running water. Curtis Brasher and at least one investigator believed the water was used to clean a bloodied floor.

Other theories included speculation that Dan Brasher had killed the Dyes and then left town in Billy's old Ford, or that the three men left together.

Hope lived on that someone, somewhere, would come forward with new information. At one point, officers talked with a dying man who, they felt sure, knew what had happened to the three missing men. They sat down by his bed and listened to his rattling cough of tuberculosis, knowing he had only a short time to live. They pleaded their case, then waited in the hall while the man mulled over what they had said.

"No, I think I'll just die and take it with me," the man told them.

Desperate for the information they knew the man possessed, they tried another tactic.

"Would you want to die with that on your conscience?" they asked him.

"Hell, yes," the man answered. "I ain't gonna tell nobody!"

Several days later, the man lapsed into a coma and died. Whatever knowledge he may have had died with him.

While the interest of the public and law enforcement personnel waxed and waned with the hope and disappointment of false leads, Curtis Brasher refused to give up. He lived and breathed the case, even dreaming about caves and mine shafts when he slept. He called sheriff's deputies regularly and made trips to their offices, asking if they had new leads and sharing his own. He called newspaper reporters, went to Montgomery several times, and fired off more letters, trying to keep the case from fading into the archives of unsolved murders.

Out of sheer desperation, in the late 1960s Brasher began sifting through all the evidence that had accumulated, hoping to find a clue he might have missed. He decided to focus on an early 1960s report by a Blount County man who said he had seen someone burying a car with a bulldozer the night the trio disappeared.

The location, he said, was just off Alabama 79 north of Pinson, where a railroad overpass bridge was under construction at the time. Pinson is not that far from Morris, Brasher reasoned, so it was not inconceivable that the trio had been entombed in their Ford under the highway.

It took Brasher a year to locate the Blount County man. Brasher convinced state officials to give the man a lie-detector test, which indicated he was telling the truth. This led to some drilling in 1969 at the reported site, where the man remembered seeing the bulldozer working.

Unfortunately, the drilling raised nothing but rocks, dirt and more false hopes.

The man took Brasher to the site in April, 1972, and died of a heart attack later that same day. Fortunately, he had drawn a crude map, which he also gave Brasher. Curtis Brasher became convinced that the man was telling the truth when he said he had seen the bulldozer dig a hole, push a car in and run back and forth over the car, crushing it, before covering the hole.

The man had said he was headed for work at a Birmingham plant in the pre-dawn hours of March 4, 1956, when he witnessed the mysterious scenario.

Besides the Blount County man, a highway construction worker had reported that a piece of heavy equipment parked near the embankment construction site had been moved during the night that the trio disappeared.

Brasher badgered authorities about testing the site once more. On his side this time was Ed Strickland, director of the Commission to Preserve the Peace. Between them, they persuaded Tom Gloor, a new county commissioner, to probe again the ground just north of the Pinson railroad overpass.

Bolstered by an ex-convict's statement that only two of the three men were in the car, and that a double-barrel shotgun would be found with them, Gloor felt there was enough new evidence to warrant further investigation. And when a sophisticated sonar device indicated a large mass of metal about 18 feet long and 14 feet underground, at a different site than the 1969 borings, Gloor asked the state Highway Department to do some more test boring. As a favor to Gloor, district engineer Clyde T. White agreed to the tests.

"My main purpose in this is not to be any hero or try to uncover something that no one has been able to do in 16 years, but to clear the air once and for all and to put the minds of the family of these men to rest on whether or not the car and bodies of their relatives are in fact there," Gloor told newspaper reporters.

White's crew began drilling November 2 into an embankment leading up to the railroad overpass. They sank holes at staggered five-foot intervals for a stretch of almost 200 feet along the highway's shoulder.

While Curtis Brasher was ecstatic over the renewed interest in the case, he was disappointed over the digging site.

"I'm glad they're digging again, but they're in the wrong spot," he told reporters on the scene.

Brasher believed the car was buried several hundred yards north of the dig site, and so did a private investigator who had worked on the case for four years.

After 16 years of searching, it seemed that the first solid clue in the case was found. Two days into the drilling, the highway crew hit a cavity about 25 feet below the surface. The drill brought up several metal fragments, and another drilling five feet away produced more fragments. Among them was a piece about two inches long and made of brass, according to Curtis Brasher.

"In my estimation, they were pieces of automotive material," he said.

Marion Dye, the 72-year-old father of the missing Dye boys, was on the scene when the metal was pulled up.

"I've put in more than eight years on this now," he said of the search for his relatives.

A preliminary toxicologist's report said it was "questionable but possible" that the fragments came from an automobile. The report also said the fragments could have come from a car's muffler.

Gloor cautioned that the metal might not be from a car at all, but he felt there was enough of a possibility to warrant digging up the embankment. He took his findings to Alabama State Investigators in Montgomery, who agreed to re-open the case.

On November 13, with anxious Dye-Brasher relatives looking on and curious spectators lined up for a quarter of a mile, Jefferson County mining experts began tunneling into the side of the embankment. Their goal was 33 feet into the hill, at a spot almost directly beneath the edge of the pavement. They used picks and shovels, so that any evidence turned up would not be destroyed by the digging.

Meanwhile, threats against Commissioner Gloor and some of his employees strengthened the belief that incriminating evidence would be found. Gloor himself received three threatening telephone calls, and an employee connected with the drilling activity said his family did, too.

A fifth threat was delivered in person to another county employee, who, as it turned out, was not involved with the searching operations. A man went to the Ensley area home of the employee and warned his wife that her husband "better not have anything to do with the Pinson job" if he wanted his family to stay alive.

Eight days after the digging began, a 40-foot shaft 48 inches in diameter invaded the embankment. The tunnel was all the way through the spot where the metal mass was supposed to be. In fact, it had passed through all three drill holes, and when workers probed the last drill hole, no traces of metal were found.

The only ray of hope in an otherwise dismal operation was the traces of oil found in some of the soil. Oil does not deteriorate over time, and speculation ran rampant that the oil found in the tunnel could have come from an automobile. On the other hand, it could have come from any of the heavy machinery working on the highway construction in 1956, the drilling crew said.

Finding the oil led workers to wonder whether they had miscalculated and tunneled below their target. This caused Gloor to order saturation drilling, which amounted to punching holes in the shoulder of the road every few inches, in an effort to relocate the mass.

"We're going to pull out all the stops," Gloor said.

Another week went by, and hopes faded a little

more with each setting sun. Workers even lowered a television camera—the type used by county workmen to find leaks and breaks in sewers—into some of the drill holes. Relatives were allowed to view the picture, but all they saw was blackness.

"It's like looking for a needle in a haystack," said Gloor. "And we're not even sure we're in the right haystack."

In a last-ditch effort to unearth the metal mass, Gloor called in a backhoe two weeks after the original probing began. Four 30-inch-wide trenches, nine feet apart and 23-feet deep, were cut into the embankment. No car was found.

By this time, public interest in the search had died. The hundreds of spectators who watched the first few days of digging had moved on, and cars whizzed by the scene, their drivers oblivious to what was happening. Only a few relatives remained. Of course, Curtis Brasher was among them.

"I'm the one that's been after them all these years," said Brasher, who was 41 when his cousins disappeared. "I'm going to have to be satisfied. There's a car buried in this fill. How they're going to find it, I don't know."

Marion Dye stood in the mud, a sad look in his tired eyes as he watched the workmen go methodically about their business.

"If there ain't nothing there, they're going to have to stop digging, I reckon," Dye said, his eyes damp from the cold and his dashed hopes of giving his sons a proper burial. "It's been 16 years and eight months now. If they don't find anything today, then this might be the end of it now and forever."

Tom Gloor decided that was to be the end of it. Three weeks after the search began, he called a halt to the digging. Within a couple of weeks, the embankment was re-sodded, leaving no trace of the digging, much less of the hopes, prayers and tears that had accompanied it. Other than a few bits of metal, a piece of rubber and some oil-stained soil, the efforts had produced nothing. Yet Gloor felt satisfied that he had done his best to give a little peace to the Dye-Brasher relatives.

"I think we have cleared up something that has been in the minds of people in this area for 16 years now," he said. "I am satisfied that the car is not there and the family is, too."

Perhaps Gloor was satisfied, but Curtis Brasher was not.

"I'll never give up, not as long as I'm living," the 56-year-old mechanic told newspaper reporters.

Brasher remained true to his word. He continued to tramp across hundreds of miles of wilderness when everyone else, including his own family, urged him to give it up as a hopeless cause. By 1973 Brasher, a ninth-grade dropout and father of four, had logged more than 100,000 miles checking out leads from one end of this state to the other, and a few out of state.

"The Lord just didn't mean for them boys to be treated like that," he would tell people. "And I'm bound to find them boys or spend the rest of my life trying."

Most folks thought the 1972 digging would put the case to rest. Two years later, however, Gloor received some new information that renewed his interest in the case. Although he would not say what the evidence was, it prompted him to meet with state investigators and to call in the U.S. Navy. In the summer of 1975, the Navy searched the area around the Alabama 79 overpass near Pinson with magnetic devices, and told Gloor that there was a 3,500 pound object on the south side of the bridge.

More tests uncovered only a small piece of metal, so investigators decided to try the north side of the bridge, near where the 1972 digging had occurred. Gloor halted traffic in the area, more holes were bored, and the magnetic division of the Naval Coastal Systems Laboratory at Panama City, Florida, brought in a magnetometer and other equipment to measure signals down in the holes.

"There is very little doubt there is a magnetic target 25 feet below the surface of the road," said Dr. Kenneth Allen, head of the division. "Our measurements on the surface indicated this and in order to be sure, we drilled down 20 feet. We don't know what it is, but the measurements are consistent with it being the target."

When investigators announced that the Navy believed there was a metal mass under the road, a chorus of doxologies rose up in the Dye-Brasher families. Hopes for finding the men soared. Once again, Curtis Brasher watched the drilling and digging operation closely, convinced that his years of playing detective would at last be vindicated.

"I know the car is in the road," Brasher said. "And with all this good equipment they're bound to find it."

Unlike the previous dig, when sheriff's deputies had stood around the excavation site grumbling about having to be there and offering considerable skepticism that anything would be found, almost everyone involved in the case felt it would be solved when the object was uncovered.

Simmering controversy over who was heading the search bubbled to the surface long before anything else, however.

Sheriff Mel Bailey contended that the case was his jurisdiction, but his responsibility and authority as primary investigator in the case were being circumvented by Gloor.

"Nobody contacted me for a look at the file," Bailey told a reporter doing a recap of the Dye-Brasher case several years later. "They just took somebody's wild guess. The sheriff's department has never drilled or dug that highway. We had the file, and there was just no basis for doing that."

Sources told *The Birmingham News* that the Sheriff's Department had been left out on purpose, for fear that someone "might mess up the case." Once again, concern was expressed that perhaps someone, for some reason, did not want the case solved. It was a persistent accusation that rankled Sheriff Bailey.

Apparently, the situation was ironed out. After several days of drilling, all investigators, as well as Gloor and County Commissioner Chriss Doss, committed themselves to digging up whatever was underneath the highway. After all, the possibility of arrests in the case still remained, because there is no statute of limitations on murder.

Emotions ran high on December 13, 1975, when 100 to 150 pounds of twisted metal was dug out of a huge hole. A collective sigh of relief went up. At last, the missing Ford had been found, many felt.   The metal was sent to a laboratory for testing. With great expectations, investigators, the Dye-Brasher family, and the general public awaited the verdict. Hopes were dashed once again, however, when the metal turned out to be a piece of culvert pipe.

With heads hanging low, officials called off the digging and refilled the 35-foot-deep hole. The road was repaved and reopened, and traffic resumed.

"I am genuinely sorry that we didn't find what we were looking for," Gloor said. "I think this will finish the search, at least in that area. If it is resumed somewhere else, it will have to be with someone else's involvement rather than mine."

As another chapter in the long search ended, several people joined Brasher in his criticism of the Sheriff's Department's investigative efforts. One was Tom Ellison, an early investigator who had devoted much of his spare time to the case.

The retired deputy told a newspaper reporter that five years after the three men disappeared, about 1,600 people from north Jefferson County signed a petition asking that he be placed on the case. At that time Ellison had a reputation for solving spectacular criminal cases.

Ellison said then-Sheriff McDowell finally agreed, but refused to allow him access to any investigative files that had been accumulated.

"On my own, I trailed the case from Sardis to Robinwood to here," Ellison said in 1975, as he stood near where the third digging took place. "I know where they were killed. I know who saw it. I know who did it. I got right up to that point, and I was taken off the case."

Ellison said he was transferred to another part of the county by McDowell and told to stay off the Dye-Brasher case. He also accused Sheriff Bailey, while campaigning for office in the early 1960s, of leaving some people of north Jefferson County under the impression that he would return Ellison to the case if he became sheriff. Once elected, Bailey gave Ellison a job outside criminal investigation in the western area.

Bailey said he did promise a number of people that he would do all he could to solve the case, but that he never promised to put Ellison back on it. He said the subject never even came up between him and the deputy.

"You've finally got to justify a continuing action with no results," said Bailey, who had inherited the case from former Sheriff McDowell. "How long are we going to keep hammering away at this thing? There are a lot more serious cases still unsolved. I wish someone would show an interest in *them*."

Talk died down after the third unsuccessful dig. People occasionally called Gloor with new information, but he had neither the manpower nor the time to investigate. He told *Birmingham Post-Herald* reporter Kathy Kemp in 1984 that he was no longer convinced a car was under Alabama 79, and was no longer in a position to find out. Gloor has since died.

Kemp's article also quoted retired Lt. O.M. Rains,

who had headed the state investigation in the case, as saying he was certain the highway held the answer to the men's disappearance.

"I'll go to my grave knowing who killed them and where the bodies are," Rains reiterated.

He always believed that the Dye brothers died March 3, 1956, in a brawl at the party, and that their bodies were buried under Alabama 79. He also said Dan Brasher was killed a few days later because he had witnessed his cousins' deaths. Rains and several others believed that the killers probably buried Brasher's body in a grave in a Morris cemetery.

In that same 1984 article, Sheriff Bailey said a grave in a Morris-Majestic area cemetery was searched after his department got word it contained two bodies.

"We satisfied ourselves that that wasn't the case," he said.

The case attracted little attention over the next five or six years. But in the fall of 1981, a self-described ex-whiskey runner came forward, claiming Billy and Robert Dye and Dan Brasher got caught stealing moonshine from a cave in Blount County. After they were shot, he said, their killer sealed off that part of the cave with a dynamite blast.

The moonshiner went so far as to take a lawman and a *Birmingham News* reporter to the cave, where he introduced another man, who said Brasher gave him a gallon of moonshine the night he disappeared. He said Brasher confided that it was filched from a moonshiner's stash in the Blount County woods, found when he and the Dyes were hunting.

The lawman discovered the sole of an old shoe in the cave, hardened by the mineral water dripping on it for years, but it did not prove to be a new clue.

Still another twist in the story surfaced in June, 1984, when a man named T.J. Chamblee told police in Abbeville, Louisiana, that he had killed Dan Brasher and Robert and Billy Dye that rainy night in 1956.

When confronted by Jefferson County Sheriff's Capt. Donald Haynes, however, Chamblee denied having participated in the killings. He told Haynes he never even witnessed the killings, but that someone had told him about them and where the bodies were buried.

"He told me he didn't do it and didn't recall saying he did," Capt. Haynes said. "He said he might have said that when he was drunk." Abbeville police confirmed that Chamblee was drunk when he confessed to the killings.

Chamblee told Haynes that his cousin, who was dead by that time, had killed the missing men and told him where the bodies were hidden. He also described an area in north Jefferson County where the bodies could be found. Officials refused to disclose the location, however, and no digging was done.

"We never could locate the specific site this fellow was trying to tell us about," Haynes said. "He said that's where the bodies would be, or that's what he was told. But now we're talking about third-hand information."

Haynes said Chamblee told him at one point the bodies were in a mine, and later that the bodies were in an air shaft. An air shaft, though, is an opening to a mine.

"That area around Trafford and Warrior is full of mine shafts," said Haynes, who is retired now. "Back then (1956), a lot of families ran their own mines. They used mules to carry out the ore. Unless you've got specific or very good information, you could spend the rest of your life just looking in those little old mine shafts."

By the mid-1980s, even though the case had possessed him for almost 30 years, Curtis Brasher said he was tired of chasing down information that led to nowhere. In 1984, with his body racked with the last stages of cancer and his spirit broken, he finally admitted defeat.

"I believe Dan's over there in that mine where the hair was found," Brasher told reporter Kathy Kemp. "I believe there's a car under that road there in Pinson, and I believe the Dye boys are probably in it. I think someday somebody will come forward. It's got to be a lot on a fellow's mind to do something like that."

Curtis Brasher spent nearly half his life searching for his three cousins. He often said he did not want to die without knowing what had happened. But a year after his last interview, Brasher lost his battle with cancer. He was buried on April 19, 1985.

The mystery of his relatives' disappearance has never been solved.

The disappearance of the Dye brothers and their cousin on March 4, 1956, is one of the most baffling cases ever recorded by Jefferson County lawmen. Caves and mine shafts have been explored, highways bored and dug up over the years...but no identifiable trace of the men or...car has ever been found.

Photo of John Dijt. His disappearance along with yacht and friends remains a Gulf of Mexico mystery.

The Case Of The Flying Dutchman

One of the most bizarre and intriguing mysteries of the high seas involves the disappearance of an Alabama-owned yacht in waters off the Florida Panhandle. The story combines the elements of an old-fashioned murder mystery with those of a modern-day movie thriller. But with no bodies and only circumstantial evidence to go on, even Sherlock Holmes would have a tough time separating truth from rumor to solve the case.

John Dijt, owner of the yacht, lived the American dream. In 1971, this 39-year-old native of Amsterdam, Holland, was president and CEO of three U.S. corporations, including Thermal Components Inc., of Montgomery, Alabama. Thermal Components was a research and development company that was gearing up to produce heat exchange surfaces that Dijt had invented. Originally aimed at the air conditioning and refrigeration industries, the devices eventually were directed toward the automotive industry.

Invention came easily for the tall, personable Dijt, who became a U.S. citizen in 1969 and an avowed Alabamian before that. He had designed and built the air conditioning ground-support system for the F-111 jet aircraft, and for the missile tracking station on the island of Antigua.

In February, 1973, Dijt started construction on a 109,000-square foot building to house Thermal Components in Montgomery's Gunter Industrial Park. He had already bought out two Buffalo, N.Y., companies in allied businesses, one that manufactured the machinery and equipment he needed to make the heat exchangers, and another that made thin-walled tubing.

By 1976, the business was doing well. Dijt, who loved the sea, was able to buy a 47-foot pleasure boat. He christened it "The Flying Dutchman," never suspecting that it was to become as legendary as its namesake. In traditional sea lore, The Flying Dutchman was a ghost ship whose captain was condemned to sail the seas eternally, without ever coming into port, as punishment for a crime.

In October, 1976, Dijt, then 44, told his wife, Carolyn, that he wanted to take the pleasure boat to Fort Lauderdale, Florida, and that he would be back in Montgomery on November 2. He wanted to sell The Dutchman and look around for a bigger boat.

The Dutchman was docked behind the Miramar Hotel in Fort Walton Beach, Florida, where Dijt kept a room. Terry Stone, a 46-year-old retired Air Force major and a close friend, lived in Fort Walton and kept an eye on the boat for Dijt. On Monday, October 25, The Dutchman left Fort Walton carrying Dijt and Stone, along with Jeanne Fontenot Kelly, the 46-year-old widow of a Destin, Florida, millionaire, and Ruth Easterly, a businesswoman from Greenville, Mississippi

The Stones knew Mrs. Kelly. Terry and his wife, Nancy, had introduced Jeanne to her late husband, Coleman Kelly, according to Mrs. Stone.

"I think Jeanne wanted to go down to south Florida, and Ruth probably said she would go along to keep Jeanne company," Mrs. Stone says.

Dijt called his wife the night he left Fort Walton Beach, and told her that someone had been threatening him with a knife.

He said he could not elaborate because someone was listening to their conversation.

"We've got trouble on our hands," he was quoted as saying. "I will call later and tell you everything."

He may have had a mechanical problem, too. Newspaper accounts indicate his oil gauge had given him trouble on a prior trip. Nancy Stone, who was on board The Dutchman the night before it left Fort Walton, says that the boat had electrical problems twice before it finally left.

Robert Neyendorf, a former Fort Walton Beach police detective who investigated The Flying Dutchman case, discounts the idea that The Dutchman was less than seaworthy, however.

"I interviewed a local man who did work on The Dutchman, and he said it was in first class shape when it left Fort Walton," Neyendorf says.

Reports regarding where The Dutchman docked that night are cloudy, too. Initial newspaper articles said it tied up in Panama City, but information later uncovered by Neyendorf, who got involved in the case at the request of police in Montgomery, says the Dutchman docked in Panama City only for the afternoon, then went on to Apalachicola, a small Panhandle town about 60 miles east of Panama City.

Neyendorf offers as evidence an interview with a waitress who witnessed a fight on board The Dutchman its last night in port.

"It was at the Rainbow Marina and Hotel in Apalachicola, where you walked right out of this restaurant and onto the dock," says Neyendorf, who was a police sergeant at the time of the disappearance. "There was a disturbance on board late at night, the waitress said. She called the sheriff's department, and a deputy came out, but he didn't file a report. The next day, the boat disappeared."

The four Dutchman passengers reportedly partied aboard the boat that night, then left port the next morning via the Intracoastal Waterway. At 2:48 p.m., the vessel passed under the John Gorrie bridge at Apalachicola, headed for the open waters of the Gulf of Mexico.

The Flying Dutchman was never heard from again.

When Mrs. Dijt reported the vessel missing, Coast Guard and Air Force search teams swung into action. As many as 13 airplanes and three ships took part in a week-long search that covered 45,000 square miles between Cape San Blas and Key West.

High winds and seas hampered the search during part of that time, and the search teams burned $100,000 worth of fuel. They found no trace of The Flying Dutchman or any of its passengers.

During the first few days after The Dutchman's disappearance, Mrs. Stone talked to Mrs. Dijt several times by telephone. Mrs. Dijt was quite worried, but Mrs. Stone says she just knew the boat was safe.

"A lot of these little towns along the coast close up for the winter, and I kept telling her not to worry, they probably just couldn't get to a phone to call us," she recalls. "The Air Force flew a grid to search for the boat, and I kept thinking, 'They have the technology to read the brand name on a bicycle while flying over Russia. Surely they can find a boat in the Gulf.'"

Throughout the searches, Mrs. Stone says she kept thinking it was impossible for anything to happen to Terry on The Flying Dutchman.

"He had been a fighter pilot in the Air Force," she recalls. "In Guam, he had a flame-out on takeoff, which is pretty serious, and in upper Michigan he was flying a light plane and the engine quit. I figured there was no way he could survive all of that, then get on a boat and get lost. So all I could think about was whether he had enough cigarettes and if he was cold."

The disappearance of the vessel attracted the attention of George Wallace, who was governor of Alabama at the time, and his wife, Cornelia, who was an acquaintance of Dijt's. Gov. Wallace put the state marine police on alert. Flyers describing The Flying Dutchman were distributed to marinas along the state's Gulf Coast, and Mrs. Wallace attended a top-level meeting in Washington concerning the disappearance.

Marijuana smuggling by boat between Florida and South America was rampant in those days, and people started talking about modern-day pirates and hijackings. Law enforcement authorities distributed flyers warning yachtsmen against getting too friendly with people aboard strange vessels, and some yachtsmen started carrying weapons.

The story took several bizarre twists over the next few months, with red herrings and dead-end leads popping up in several places. For example:

• On February 11, 1977, a bottle found floating in Santa Rosa Sound, west of Fort Walton Beach, contained a cryptic message.

"Flying Dutchman. 3 Cubans on board. Help. Headed due east," a note inside said.

The FBI laboratory in Washington checked the bottle, and revealed that the note was written on cheap, blue-lined school notebook paper. The agency pronounced it a fake.

"The bottle and note couldn't have gotten to where it did without going against the current," an FBI agent said.

Robert Neyendorf is not so sure.

"I got samples of Terry Stone and John Dijt's handwriting, and sent them, along with the note, to a local handwriting expert," he says. "She said the handwriting in the note was similar to that of Terry Stone."

Neyendorf also showed the note paper to Nancy Stone, who said it was similar to a notepad her husband had on board The Flying Dutchman.

"That bottle was found one mile west from where The Dutchman docked in Fort Walton, and the normal tide would have carried it that far," Neyendorf contends.

• A Minnesota businessman visiting Panama City in April, 1977, reported having heard The Dutchman's radio distress signal the day it disappeared. He said he did not report it at the time because he was having problems with his own boat, and assumed others had heard the mayday call, too. Although law enforcement authorities took his statement, the information did not pan out.

• A citizens band radio operator in New York claimed that on May 23, 1977—seven months after The Dutchman's disappearance—he talked via short-wave radio with a Dutchman passenger named Terry, who claimed he was alive and living in Honduras.

• A car rental billed to one of the women who had been on board The Flying Dutchman looked like a break in the case. It turned out to be a simple billing error unrelated to her disappearance.

Over the next few years, the investigation took a back seat to other pressing matters. No concrete evidence about the yacht's fate turned up. To all appearances, it had simply vanished, swallowed up by the sea. Families of the four missing passengers got on with their lives, and learned to cope with the loss of their loved ones. A court declared Jeanne Kelly officially dead in November, 1981, clearing the way for her seven children to settle her estate. In October, 1989, Terry Stone was declared legally dead, too. A probate judge in

Montgomery, Alabama, had already ruled in February, 1977, that John Dijt had died accidentally at sea. Then, seven years after The Flying Dutchman sailed into the sunset, a late-night telephone call from a remorseful sea captain reopened old wounds.

"I've got to talk to somebody right now," the captain said in a July, 1983, phone call to Robert Neyendorf. "I've had this on my conscience for six years. I've got reason to believe The Flying Dutchman was hijacked. The four persons on board were killed and thrown overboard."

The call stunned Neyendorf, by then a lieutenant with the Fort Walton Beach Police Department. Although he wanted desperately to find the missing yacht, Neyendorf had just about given up hope. This new information, unlike the pranks and false leads in the past, offered a ray of hope that the pleasure boat's fate might still be determined.

The sea captain said he and three other people, including a Key West businesswoman, saw The Flying Dutchman in Honduras three months after it vanished. The captain, who immediately became a prime suspect, acknowledged he was a wanted man who had skippered a drug smuggling ship himself. Speaking as if he had been aboard The Dutchman when the murders took place, the captain said he heard The Dutchman's occupants say they were looking for diesel fuel to deliver the boat to Panama. The Key West businesswoman, who was never publicly identified, later confirmed the captain's story. The other two witnesses were dead.

"There is every indication he knew what happened," Neyendorf said at the time of the call. "I believe he might have had something to do with it."

When Neyendorf was on the phone with the captain, the policeman elicited the seaman's name and Social Security number.

The Fort Walton Beach radio operator punched it

into the National Crime Information Center (NCIC) computers, which showed he was who he said he was, and that he was wanted on a federal charge for boat hijacking.

The sea captain, whom Neyendorf identifies as "Roy," gave Neyendorf enough details to convince the veteran police officer that he really knew what he was talking about. Roy said he saw The Dutchman docked on a little island called Roatan, off the coast of Honduras.

"I asked him, was he sure it was The Dutchman, and he said yes, it had been repainted, but he was experienced enough to recognize when a boat had been painted, the way a car dealer can tell if a car has been repainted," Neyendorf says. "He said he knew the boat, and recognized its fiberglass dingy on the foredeck. He said Dijt's gold-colored rods and reels were still attached to the boat, and that its electrical outlet was on the left instead of the right, where it would normally be located, which was true of The Dutchman. He said he saw some guys loading yellow barrels onto the boat."

One of the witnesses the sea captain said was with him in Honduras was a "very, very reputable society lady from Key West, Florida," who verified Roy's story.

"She vowed to deny the story if anyone else questioned her, but she said that yes, she and Roy had been sitting in a restaurant that evening on the island when two guys — Cubans or South Americans — talked of getting diesel fuel to take the boat to Panama. She said she didn't know The Dutchman, but that Roy obviously did, and that it was all she could do to keep him from boarding it. The next morning, the boat was gone."

Neyendorf was never able to get back in touch with the sea captain.

"He told me he was calling from Fort Myers, but I knew it was a local call," Neyendorf says.

The sea captain also gave Neyendorf the names of two men he said hijacked The Dutchman.

"My notes show them, and the name of the north Florida fishing village where they lived," Neyendorf says.

The notes he refers to are part of his private papers. His official files on the case are mysteriously missing.

"I had a two-inch file at the police department, and when I checked a year or so ago, I was told it wasn't there," he says.

The same night the remorseful Roy called Robert Neyendorf, he also disturbed Nancy Stone's sleep. He told her a story similar to what he told Neyendorf, but Mrs. Stone was so flustered she did not ask many questions and therefore did not get as much information as the police lieutenant.

"He (Roy) called me one night and told me, 'I'd know that boat anywhere, and you've been on my conscience lately,' " recalls Mrs. Stone, a real estate agent in Fort Walton. "But 'on my conscience' means 'on my mind.' That's the way they talk in south Louisiana. It doesn't mean he was involved in The Dutchman's disappearance, as the police seemed to think. I don't think he was. He told me he had been in Honduras and that he had seen the boat. I never heard from him again."

Mrs. Stone says she met a sea captain named Roy once, but she cannot say for sure it was the same man who called her. She feels like it was, though, and still hopes to hear from him again someday. The Roy she met was a drifter whose last name she never knew.

"Terry told me he (Roy) was from Louisiana, where he had been in trouble with the law, maybe even broke out of prison, I'm not sure," she says. "I think Terry had gone shrimping with him, but the only time I ever saw him was when he came to our house one time and I answered the door. I went into the kitchen while he was there."

About a year after the old sea captain's calls to

Neyendorf and Nancy Stone, reports began to surface
that Dijt was still alive and in hiding. A private investigator, who had been pursuing the case for several
years as a hobby, claimed to have interviewed several
people who had seen Dijt in recent months.

A Fort Walton newspaper article stating that
Dijt's company was the subject of a federal investigation at the time of his disappearance appeared to add
credence to speculation that Dijt had disappeared on
purpose. The article said that documents obtained by
the newspaper under the Freedom of Information Act
indicated a federal investigation, focusing on the al-
leged misuse of government funds, had begun 24 days
before The Flying Dutchman vanished.

Even a spokesman for Dijt's insurance company,
Mutual of New York, acknowledged that there was a lot
of circumstantial evidence suggesting Dijt might still
be alive, according to newspaper articles.

But Robert Neyendorf says the various "sightings" of
Dijt, including those in an Atlanta, Georgia, bar, proved
to be false. As for the investigation into Thermal Components, it ended in January, 1977, with Dijt and his
company being cleared of any financial wrongdoing.

Truman Hobbs, now a U.S. district judge in Montgomery, represented the Dijt family as a private attorney at the time of The Dutchman's disappearance. Like
others close to the case, he is convinced foul play was
involved.

"Someone hijacked the boat and killed them," he
told *The Mobile Press Register* in 1992. The idea that all
four people aboard would just decide to take off was
"preposterous," he said, making a pretty good case for
his view. "One of the ladies had a small child at home.
John Dijt's son was going to be naturalized the following week."

He pointed out that Terry Stone, The Dutchman's
skipper, had a wife and three children. Mrs. Kelly was
a widow and the mother of seven children, the youngest

then just three. Mrs. Easterling was a widow with two adult sons.

Hobbs said he suspected that whoever took the boat lay in wait for it at one of the Panhandle ports, killed the foursome and used the boat for several drug smuggling runs. He said it was "highly unlikely" that the boat met with an accident.

In a more recent interview, Hobbs could not recall any federal investigation involving Thermal Components.

"I was the company's attorney, I would have known about it," he says. "If they had started an investigation, I can see why they would determine it was a waste of time. The company had turned the corner by the time he (Dijt) disappeared, and was doing well. It was finally sold for over $26 million."

There was other evidence that the four were dead, too. Dijt was carrying $1,000 in travelers' checks, which never were cashed.

Robert Neyendorf, who went on to become Fort Walton Beach's police chief before retiring in 1985, agrees with the foul play scenario. Firmly convinced the boat was hijacked at a Florida port, he points to the mysterious phone call Dijt made to his wife the day before he disappeared, and notes unconfirmed reports that other people got on the boat before it left the Panhandle.

"What happens is this: Dope smugglers will hijack a boat if it's seaworthy, make a couple of runs between South America and Florida, then abandon it because it's hot," Neyendorf says today from his home in Fort Walton. "Smugglers are known to hijack boats like these because they're fast and seaworthy. I'm firmly convinced that's what happened to The Flying Dutchman."

During the early months of the investigation, a Coast Guard official in Washington admitted there was a "very strong possibility" the yacht was seized by

high-seas hijackers, and that those aboard were mur-
dered. He said the department's active file on missing
vessels showed that at least 38 vanished without a
trace from U.S. waters between 1971 and 1977.

He said 12 of those, including The Flying Dutchman, were listed as possible hijackings.

The case of The Flying Dutchman has been closed
now for several years, but recent developments could
see it reopened.

In April, 1991, scuba divers Robert Speidel of
Tallahassee, Florida, and Harry Andrews of Carrabelle,
a small town about 80 miles east of Panama City,
located what they thought was a sunken shrimp boat
45 miles southeast of Carrabelle. In May, 1991, the
wreckage was identified by the Florida Marine Patrol
as that of The Pirate's Lady, a yacht that vanished in
the Gulf about three months after The Flying
Dutchman's disappearance.

With the positive identification of The Pirate's
Lady, Andrews began to ponder another, similar wreckage he had discovered several years earlier. Located
about 50 miles from the charred remains of The Lady,
in the path from Apalachicola to Tarpon Springs, that
earlier discovery may be The Flying Dutchman,
Andrews believes.

"I just thought it was another old wreck at the
time," Andrews says of his discovery. "I was spear
fishing, and I was using an underwater sonar device to
locate fish when I found it."

When he did put two and two together, he could
not come up with four, because he could not remember
where the wreck was located. That is why he could not
go back until 1993.

"I had put my Loran numbers in a book in code, so
no one else could read them," says Andrews, speaking
of the device that takes radio signal readings to place
a site. "Then I forgot the code. I went back one year, but
I couldn't find the wreck. I couldn't figure out what was

going on. When I finally translated my code, I went right to it."

He says he only dove the site three or four times, but the last two times he found a sport fishing wheel in the debris field.

"That's what made me think it was something besides an old shrimper," he says.

In the spring of 1994, Andrews went out with the Florida Marine Patrol to try and salvage enough pieces to positively identify the boat. However, the waters were so rough he had to turn back about five miles from shore.

"Next time, we'll spend all day searching the area for clues and videotaping what we find," he says, the excitement evident in his voice. "I'm expecting good clear water and visibility next time. I should be able to tell for sure if it's The Flying Dutchman. I really believe it is."

Even if Andrews is right, his discovery may not solve the mystery of how The Flying Dutchman disappeared. The sea clings tenaciously to its murky secrets.

The Mystery Of The Crying Pecan Tree

Deep within the Choctaw County backwoods, high on a hill in the Shady Grove community near Needham, Linnie Jenkins lives in a three-bedroom, frame house on land homesteaded by her maternal grandparents. Honeysuckle, roses, and wildflowers dot the meadows of the Wes Busby plantation each spring, as wild rabbits hop through the rolling woods and the buds of peach, pear, apple, fig, and plum trees open their eager faces to the sky.

Like most of the men in this small, rural county, Linnie Jenkins's father and grandfather logged for pulp wood and raised corn, peas, beans, okra, cucumbers, tomatoes, and children.

Linnie, who has been separated from her husband, A.J. Jenkins, since 1980, still grows most of the food she eats, canning the excess for her winter cupboard. Nothing is wasted, right down to the shells of her peas, which she turns into pea-hull jelly. It is not an exciting existence, but it does offer a certain peace and tranquillity.

During the spring of 1981, that tranquillity was temporarily shattered by the attentions of local, state, and national news media, and by a stream of 25,000 visitors to the Jenkins farm.

From the middle of April until the end of July, Choctaw County boasted a star, an Andy Warhol example of everyone's 15 minutes of fame. The focus of this brief celebrity was an ordinary pecan tree that did something quite extraordinary—it cried.

The furor began on Palm Sunday, while five of the inhabitants of the Jenkins house—Linnie, her son and his wife, Larry Plummer and his mother—were enjoying a friendly game of cards. About 8:30 p.m., while the unrelated boy Linnie raised was asleep in the back bedroom, the tree began its mournful dirge.

"We didn't pay it much attention at first, because it sounded like a dog whimpering," Mrs. Jenkins recalls. "You know how a dog cries out when he's sleep-dreaming? We remarked on how it must be a pretty good dream, because it was lasting so long."

There was nothing threatening about the sound, so the family went to bed.

"Next day, I got up real early, and went out to the field to hoe some peas," says Mrs. Jenkins, who remembers the series of events as if they occurred yesterday. "When I got back, we still heard that noise."

Her son had searched the grounds for the source of the noise, and was standing beside the tall, leafy pecan tree in their front yard when Mrs. Jenkins returned from the fields. As difficult as it was to believe, the crying, whimpering puppy sound was coming from the tree's upraised roots.

"We were wondering if it was hollow and some small animal had crawled inside," Mrs. Jenkins says.

They searched the yard for holes and underground tunnels that would allow an animal entrance to the tree. They found none. After sawing into the tree, they determined it was solid, through and through.

"We dug a hole in front of the tree big enough to bury a body in, then filled it back up so nobody would fall in it," Mrs. Jenkins says. "We couldn't find anything wrong. We even hit the side of the tree to see if our noise made a difference."

It did not.

Strange thoughts flitted through their minds when the Jenkinses and Plummers could find no explanation for the plaintive cries. Was the tree, which had sheltered the Busby, Presley (Linnie's maiden name) and Jenkins families for 60 years, begging for help in an unknown tongue? Did it have some kind of malevolent spirit trapped inside, searching for an exit and poised to pounce?

While the bewildered household searched for answers, a neighbor and distant cousin walked up. He heard the crying, too, and decided to contact another party for verification of his hearing and his sanity.

Fred Childers, editor of the *Choctaw Advocate*, was up to his elbows in ink and deadlines. Tempted to ignore the call about a crying pecan tree, he allowed his nose for news to take control, grabbed a notebook, and headed for the Jenkins farm.

"It sounds like a puppy, like it's crawled up in the tree and gotten stuck," Childers told his wife that evening. "You can even hear it scratching. But the tree is solid, there's no way inside the thing. I walked all around the place and I swear there is no way for anything to be inside the tree. But it's whining."

"Yes, dear, I'm sure it is," was his wife's only reply.

The following morning, Childers returned to the crying pecan tree, taking a tape recorder and most of the *Advocate* staff with him. Tommy Campbell, assistant editor, was certain his boss had been tippling the scuppernong wine. But he brought along a high frequency remote microphone in case he was wrong. Campbell placed the microphone at the base of the tree, where the sound was the strongest, and picked up a pretty good, two-minute recording of the mysterious noise.

"The sound was continuous, except that every now and then, there would be a very brief, maybe split-second pause," says Campbell, *Advocate* editor today. "I still have that tape."

Childers played the recording for Choctaw County Sheriff Donald Lolley.

"Have you ever heard anything like this?" Childers asked.

"No, and what's more, I'm not going to admit I heard it on that tape," the sheriff replied.

He became a believer, however, when he heard the sound first-hand.

Hoping to solve the mystery quickly, Childers called the Forestry Department of Auburn University and played the tape over the telephone. The experts were stupefied.

Undaunted, he persuaded Alan Bruce, a local forester who worked for American Can Company, to listen to the tree. Bruce said it was quite probable that a fungus had entered through fissures caused when the tree was struck by lightening about eighteen months earlier. The fungus could be creating metabolic gases, in the same way humans create carbon dioxide when they breathe, he said. The gases could have collected in a pocket, built pressure and made the moaning sound as they forced their way out through the fissures.

"Privately, I was glad to have a reasonable expla-nation, but I thought the theory about old Indian burial grounds and the spirits of great chiefs was a trifle more interesting," Childers wrote in the April 23, 1981, edition of the *Advocate*.

The gas theory was soon disproved by an oil company geologist who showed up with an assortment of gear and ran a battery of tests on the beleaguered woody specimen.

"Choctaw County has a lot of sandstone in it, and the sandstone frequently has air pockets or mini caves where underground streams washed it out years ago," says Tommy Campbell. "These people doing pipeline work nearby came over and drove steel rods around the tree, but found no pockets."

Thinking someone may have rigged up a tape recorder or other electronic gear inside the tree, the pipeline workers drilled a small hole and probed inside. They also X-rayed the tree, and even ran a metal detector around it.

"There wasn't a hollow spot anywhere in it, but you could put your ear up to the tree and hear that noise," says Campbell, who is just as puzzled today as he was in 1981.

Fred Childers wrote several articles about the whimpering tree, bringing a deluge of state and national news media to the county. Television stations from throughout Alabama, from WTBS in Atlanta, and from WTOK and WHTV in nearby Meridian, Mississippi, broadcast the story. The Associated Press picked it up and sent it to member newspapers. *The Birmingham News* ran a couple of articles about the phenomenon, and Paul Harvey told "the rest of the story" on his syndicated radio program.

"This thing got national television coverage, too," says Campbell. "CNN and other networks picked up on it, and the *National Enquirer* wrote a story about it."

Attracted by the publicity, a guru from California showed up on the Jenkins doorstep one morning about daylight, unannounced, to exorcise the spirits from the tree.

"When I opened my front door that morning, there stood this man dressed in white robes, with a white towel or something around his head," Mrs. Jenkins says. "It scared me to death. I thought something had come out of that tree."

The man in white, who had managed to slip

quietly past what was usually a vociferous hound, informed Mrs. Jenkins that "the Lord" had told him to "hold communion" at the tree.

"I told him to go ahead, and I went on and dusted my tomatoes," she says. "He knelt down and had prayer or something, I couldn't understand what he was saying. Then he left."

The whining sound continued.

One of the associate producers of "That's Incredible," a national television show, heard about the tree over his car radio as he drove to work. He called Fred Childers from Los Angeles to express his interest. Apparently, the left hands do not know what the right hands are up to in Tinsel Town, because others associated with the show had already nixed the idea.

"Despite the fact that we all love the story, the story editor still insists that it is not visual enough," Kathy Parsons, of Alan Landsburg Productions, wrote to Childers after he sent her an article about the tree. (Too bad it could not tap dance while it sang.)

Getting to the Jenkins place was not an easy matter, especially for an outsider, yet thousands of visitors managed to find their way over the next few weeks. From Florida, Tennessee, California, Oregon, Alaska and the Panama Canal Zone they came, first to Butler, the county seat, then eight miles south to Needham.

They wound out of Needham on a narrow paved road, then traveled another two miles up a little dirt, sand, and gravel road to the Shady Grove community.

Droves of humanity clogged the Jenkins yard at midnight on Easter eve, and 3,000 spent the holiday in an un-holy traffic jam along the one-way route, as if expecting some sort of religious experience.

"We must have had 400 people in the yard here at one time," Mrs. Jenkins says of that Easter Sunday. "I talked so much my throat hurt."

Soon, the road leading to the tree bore evidence of

heavy use. Tire tracks corrugated it like a washboard. Several times the sheriff was called to direct the flow of traffic or pull a car out of a rut in the sand.

"I had to put a rope across the road to keep people out of my yard until I got out of bed," Mrs. Jenkins says.

She did not mind the traffic, the people or the dust, however. She even forgave the kids who took some of her chickens, after they brought them back. But she was not getting any work done, and if she did not cultivate her fields, she could not eat.

So she started charging admission—$.50 for anyone over 12 years—to listen to the whining tree. The money paid for extra hands to tend her fields while she dealt with the visitors.

Almost every carload brought another explanation about the source of the noise. Some of the theories were interesting, others just plain weird. Because the sounds could be interpreted as a baby-like cry, one person suggested there were babies buried beneath the tree. Others pushed a ghost theory, insisting Mrs. Jenkins's long dead grandparents were returning to have a look at their homeplace.

"Some said it was the devil, others said it was spirits," Mrs. Jenkins says. "One man said it was a black man who had been hung in the tree, and somebody else said it was teenagers who were killed in a wreck on that road. But there's never been anything took place here to account for that noise. There's never been anyone killed here and the tree don't have a history."

Others admonished her for cutting one of the big, thick, visible roots with an electric saw.

"They said the tree was crying 'cause it was bleeding," Mrs. Jenkins says. The cuts were made after the sounds started, however.

An entomologist thought it might be either a Bess or Longhorn beetle. Both make a sound very similar to that made by the tree, he claimed. But other people who had heard those beetles said they sounded nothing like the tree, leading to the conclusion that, in this instance, at least, the entomologist was several bees short of a hive.

Writing to the *Choctaw Advocate*, a Michigan man suggested that Fred Childers climb the tree until he found a hollow. Inside, the writer assured the editor, would be a small, speckled tree frog whimpering his little green heart out.

Another letter writer bypassed all the theories and got down to business, suggesting that the Jenkinses fertilize the tree to increase its production, then sell its pecans at premium prices!

"The tale got out that a little green man with a red cap came out of the tree, and it had people looking all over the place," Mrs. Jenkins says, chuckling.

Her favorite explanation for the crying, and the most romantic, came from the person who insisted there were oceans below the tree, and that the sound was made by baby seals.

Whatever the noise was, it drove the dogs wild, according to Tommy Campbell.

"There would be a whole circle of dogs sitting around that tree with their heads cocked and their ears up, just listening," he says. "They didn't seem scared, but every now and then they would let out a howl."

All those visitors with their strange theories, all the foresters and scientists with their poking and probing, must have wearied the tree. Its attempts at communication grew weaker, and its whimpering became barely audible without the aid of a rubber hose that Linnie Jenkins pushed into its roots. Following an afternoon rain, the tree perked up and regained its former tone, only to lose it altogether for half an hour a few days later. By the end of May, the sound had grown so weak that a Mobile television show co-host had to use a stethoscope against the roots to catch the infrequent whispers.

While the tree was losing its vocal abilities, it clung tenaciously to its new-found fame. Articles and photographs still appeared in newspapers like the *Atlanta Constitution*, and in supermarket tabloids such as the *Globe* and the *Weekly World News*.

More television stations broadcast its story, and the stream of visitors continued the pilgrimage along the winding, dusty roads.

Then, just as suddenly as it had started, the sound stopped.

The tree grew silent, and has not cried since. Having received an estimated 25,000 visitors during its three months and 12 days of notoriety, it settled back into a normal routine of growing, blooming and bearing pecans. Why it ever did anything else remains a mystery.

Fyffe residents scan the skies for UFOs.

The Winter Of The UFOs

For Donna Saylor, the daylight hours of February 10, 1989, passed very pleasantly. Her sister, Cathy, and brother-in-law, Bryan, were visiting from Tennessee, and while the men fished at one of the ponds on the Saylor farm, Donna and Cathy went shopping. Their husbands caught a mess of bream for supper, and the women caught some good winter sales.

About the only wrinkle in the visit was the cold Bryan developed. His nose was red and sore, his head was stopped up, and he had a terrific headache that threatened to keep him awake all night. And there was no aspirin in the house.

"My sister and I went to Fyffe to the grocery store about 7 o'clock to get some Alka-Seltzer Plus," recalls Mrs. Saylor, a resident of the Grove Oak community near Fyffe, Alabama. "About 7:30, when we were two miles from our house, we saw this bright, white light in the sky just over the trees. We watched it as we drove home, and it didn't appear to be moving. We kept trying to figure out what it was."

Cathy commented that it must be a street light, but Mrs. Saylor pointed out that they were on top of a mountain, in a rural area that had no street lights, and with no towns or houses any higher up than their community. Besides, the closer the women got to the object, the larger it appeared. It was not until they turned off County Road 76 onto the dirt road where the Saylors live that they realized just how big it was.

"We stopped the car at a clearing at the beginning of the dirt road, about two-tenths of a mile from our house," recalls Mrs. Saylor, who had just moved into her new log home at the time. "We hadn't realized when we first spotted it that it was so close to our house. It seemed to be hovering between ours and the one across the road. It was so big, it was like viewing a satellite dish from about 50 yards away. It wasn't really round, though. It was an oblong, white light, enormously bright."

An eerie stillness enveloped the women when they turned off the car's motor. Even the crickets were silent, as if listening for any sound from the sky.

They heard nothing.

Suddenly, the light blinked out, as if a light switch had been turned off. The object vanished, instantly and noiselessly, and without so much as a vapor trail. It left two stunned women in its invisible wake.

"It just about scared my sister to death," Mrs. Saylor says. "My comment was, 'Where the heck did it go?' My sister said, 'I don't care, let's just get to the house right now.' "

More aggravated than scared, Mrs. Saylor wished she had had more time to study the object. Her thoughts were jumbled as she drove the short distance to her house, but she knew she was not crazy and she had not been hallucinating, either.

"When we got to the house, Cathy jumped out and

ran inside to tell our husbands what we had seen," Mrs. Saylor says. "They were on the couch and in the recliner, watching television."

While the men retrieved a pair of binoculars from the gun cabinet upstairs, Mrs. Saylor walked over to their pickup truck and got the two pair she and her husband used to check the livestock on the 600-acre farm they managed.

The group spotted the object again, way off in the distance.

From where they were standing, it looked like it was over Collinsville, about 20 miles southeast from Grove Oak and down off the mountain top.

"In two or three minutes, it had gone that far," Mrs. Saylor says, incredulously.

Passing the three pairs of binoculars around, the four took turns watching the object in the cold, clear, February sky.

Although they could see the object and its colored, blinking lights without the binoculars, they could not make out its shape except through the lenses.

"Everything we saw was so clear, and we watched it long enough that we had time to discuss it," Mrs. Saylor says. "It was long and had a slight curve to it, like a crescent moon. Every few minutes, it would turn, and we'd see that it had a bright light in the center, with a red light on each tip of its curve.

"When it would turn, it looked like it was spraying green lights, like they were revolving around it or down its sides. We'd say, 'Oh, look, it's doing it again, can you see those green lights?'

"We felt like it was turning away from us, and while it was turning, it looked like a big ball with green lights coming out of the bottom, kind of like fireworks."

After staring at the object for 15 to 20 minutes, Mrs. Saylor decided to call the local police and find out whether anyone else had reported the strange light show. Five minutes after she hung up the phone, the

dispatcher called Mrs. Saylor back to let her know that
the police chief and assistant chief had left to check out
her report, but might be delayed because they had
spotted the object themselves and were following it.

"She said that since I had called, she had received
other calls about the lights," Mrs. Saylor says. "We
were relieved about that. We knew we were seeing
something, and we felt better that the police took it
seriously, too."

Fyffe Police Chief Junior Garmany, a 22-year-
veteran of the force, had just returned from making his
early-evening rounds when the dispatcher took Mrs.
Saylor's call.

"Fred asked if I wanted to go with him and look for
it, and I said okay," Garmany told a newspaper reporter.

As Garmany and Assistant Chief Fred Works
drove south on Alabama 75, their car radio started
crackling. Law enforcement officers from Geraldine
and Crossville, as well as the county sheriff's department, had spotted the brightly lit object, and were
keeping each other informed as to its whereabouts.

"It's headed your way, Junior," a voice spat out of
the pastoral darkness.

Garmany and Works were somewhere in the
Gilbert's Crossroads area when they first spotted it,
and they immediately gave chase. Twelve to 15 miles
later, on County Road 43, they realized it was right up
ahead of them. They stopped, turned off the engine and
the radio, and got out of the patrol car. As the object
approached, it seemed to be large, dark and flat. It flew
right over them, without making a sound, flying so
close the men could have read its identifying marks or
numbers, had there been any.

"We figured it was going about 300 or 400 miles an
hour," Garmany told reporters.

He estimated the craft's altitude at 1,500 feet.

"It had three white lights along the bottom, shining up on itself."

Finding the object difficult to describe, Works said it was sort of triangular-shaped. Garmany described it as more of a heart shape, or similar to a stingray.

"The lights on the bottom illuminated it," he was quoted as saying. "They didn't shine down. I wasn't scared. It didn't act in an aggressive manner. If it wanted to get us, it had the drop on us. I don't know if it was from outer space, or if it was something the U.S. government was testing. But whatever it was, it wasn't a plane or a blimp or a helicopter. It was just an unidentified flying object."

When comedian James Gregory says everyone who sees UFOs lives in a mobile home, he's poking fun at a stereotypical picture held by UFO skeptics. But Garmany, Works and the Saylors are not backward country hicks who have drunk too much of their own moonshine. They are sober, literate, hard-working people who saw some strange sights that they cannot fully explain.

They were not alone.

That same Friday night, the DeKalb County Sheriff's Department received 11 calls from excited witnesses in mountainous northeast Alabama. One such call came from a Lickskillet resident who told the dispatcher, "You better get a deputy over here quick. I don't know what it is, but it's scaring the hell out of my bird dogs."

State Troopers and police officers in other DeKalb County towns also reported seeing the UFO. Like the Fyffe police, however, none of the area law enforcement agencies had an explanation. At first, they speculated about a weather balloon or a military aircraft. A check with the National Weather Service at Nashville, Tennessee, revealed that weather balloons, while sent up daily at 5 p.m. CST from various points, routinely would have burst by 7 p.m. Officials at Birmingham and Huntsville airports, Maxwell Air Force Base in

Montgomery and at the Marshall Space Flight Center
in Huntsville could add nothing to clarify the situation.

The next night produced more sightings and more
calls to the police.

"Around the same time Saturday night, or maybe
an hour later, we saw the same object again," Mrs.
Saylor reveals. "Only this time, it was in the northern
sky instead of to the southeast. That's when we thought
it might be some kind of flight out of Huntsville, but it
wasn't."

Again, she called the Fyffe police.

"I know you all will think I'm crazy, but we're
seeing that UFO again tonight," she told the dispatcher.

Fred Works and a patrolman drove out to the
Saylor house, and they saw the object again, too. By
this time, the Saylors had enlisted the aid of a neighbor
who had a telescope, so they had an even better view.

"The patrolman said it was probably a planet,"
Mrs. Saylor remembers. "I said that's fine, but an hour
ago it was over here, and planets don't travel like that."

Over the weekend, the local press called the
Saylors, and a story about the sightings appeared in a
Fort Payne daily on Monday. Larger newspapers picked
up the story, and crowds started flocking to Fyffe in
droves.

Downtown took on a carnival atmosphere for the
next few weeks, as UFO fever struck the small town
(population 1,400) like the California gold rush. Over-
enthusiastic teenage boys would whoop and point to
the sky, shouting, "There it is. It's a UFO."

Local entrepreneurs started selling UFO T-shirts,
and one night, the local fire chief built a bonfire so
people could warm their hands.

By day, callers from all over the United States lit
up the police department switchboard asking for directions. On Friday nights, traffic would be bumper-to-
bumper, with license plates from Tennessee, Georgia,

Florida and all parts of Alabama. Some nights, visitors outnumbered the locals more than two-to-one, as thousands of enthusiastic skywatchers lined the town's main thoroughfare like birds on a telephone wire. Sometimes, their vigilance was rewarded.

"It was oval or round, and it had rotating lights in the center," one woman said in describing what she saw one Friday in late February. "It was hovering in the distance, with its lights changing from green to yellow or orange." Speaking for most of the people standing around her, she added, "We were all anxious and happy. Everybody was wanting to use the binoculars."

It was the town's celestial mood that prompted the printing of the T-shirts, which depicted the UFO flying over a police car, with a red-haired officer pointing toward the sky. Fred Works just happens to have red hair. Several dozen shirts were sold for $10 each, with part of the proceeds going to the local fire department.

Others were not so generous to the local authorities, who became the butt of several jokes. After a newspaper reporter misinterpreted Mrs. Saylor's UFO description as "banana-shaped," someone stuck Christmas tree lights into a banana and hung it by a string in the police station, right over Works's desk.

"If I had known the kind of ridicule we were going to get, I'd have kept my mouth shut," said Chief Garmany. "And I'd have shot Fred if he'd opened his."

About two or three months later, when she thought all the hoopla had quieted down, Donna Saylor was stunned to see the "Fyffe banana" resurface on TV's "Good Morning, America." The program broadcast a scene from a soccer game in Australia, where a stadium full of fans wore banana-shaped, foam hats with the word "Fyffe" printed across the front.

"It blew my mind," Mrs. Saylor says. "I thought, 'What is this world coming to?'"

Later that same day, she received several calls from radio stations in London, England, whose reporters interviewed her over the air. Patiently, she answered all their questions, but when the third station called, she could not suppress her bewilderment any longer.

"I said, 'Why now? Are you that far behind on the news?'

"He said, 'Ma'am, you don't understand, this is about the Fyffe banana.'

"I said, 'Wait a minute,' and I corrected him about the crescent shape of the UFO. When I finished talking, he said, 'What kind of label do you have on your bananas?'

"I told him Chiquita and Dole. He said the bananas in England had a label that said 'Fyffe.' That's why they were so interested in the story. I couldn't help but laugh."

Over the next few weeks, at least 100 people reported seeing the UFO, some describing its white lights as "blinding."

"It went over the Rodentown community where my sister lives, and she told me later that there was such a bright white light that it lit up the inside of her house and hurt her eyes," one woman told a newspaper reporter.

Police dispatcher Shelia Smith saw the object one night, after a rescue squad worker called her to the front of the police station about 8 o'clock.

"I couldn't see a shape, but I did see the lights — red and green," she told a *Birmingham Post-Herald* reporter. "They just flickered and then went away. It's weird."

Ms. Smith, who said it was her second sighting but her first without binoculars, added that a radio station reporter spotted the UFO that same night, and that a television crew from Mobile also was at the police station when the object appeared. A gas station attendant said he saw the object flying toward nearby Geraldine.

"I called the police there and told them to go outside and look, but they said they didn't see anything," Ms. Smith said.

Teri Baker, co-owner of Rainsville's *Weekly Post* newspaper, snapped a series of four time-lapse photographs that caused a run on the issue in which it was published.

"If you look at her pictures in sequence, the object moved right to left, then up," says Carey Baker, Teri's husband and co-owner of the newspaper. "What's funny about that, I believe people who saw it remembered it moving left to right, instead. Like everything else that happened up here, I don't have any idea what that meant."

In one of the photos, there is an airplane coming across the sky, and because of the time-lapse photography, it looks like a piece of thread with knots tied in it, Carey Baker says. "The pattern of the light (UFO) and airplane were totally different," he says. "You can tell distinctly which is the aircraft. Its movement was a straight line, and the other object's wasn't."

His only personal "out of the ordinary" experience was the time he saw a spiraling light moving across the sky.

"We were fortunate enough that a fellow here videoed it," Baker says. "I thought I could probably identify the other things I saw."

Baker only printed about 1 percent of the sighting reports he heard.

"We tried to have some form of back-up before we went to press with a report — more than one, sometimes more than two people from different areas, or a group of people from one area that had seen basically the same thing," he explains.

The sightings brought national and international media attention, too. Some of it was not very flattering. The television program "Inside Edition" aired an episode on Fyffe, but many townspeople felt it poked fun at them.

Due to the number of sightings, the Mutual UFO Network (MUFON) visited the small community. Headquartered in Sequin, Texas, MUFON is an organization of mostly civilian volunteers who investigate UFO incidents that happen near their communities.

Alabama-based MUFON volunteer Jeff Ballard spent several days in Fyffe, watching the night skies and interviewing witnesses.

"At first, I thought what the people were seeing was some type of lighter-than-air military craft," says Ballard, an electrical engineer who works in Huntsville. "But when I checked, I found we're still not much farther advanced with those than we are with regular blimps."

Despite a lifelong curiosity with UFOs and six years as a MUFON investigator, Ballard has yet to have a personal sighting.

"The general rule is the UFOs are seen when Jeff Ballard is not," he jokes. But he takes other peoples' reports seriously, and keeps an open mind.

"There were a number of sightings in Fyffe, some fairly credible," he says. "There were a lot that were of the distant light type, which are hard to pin down. They could be planets or stars. But there were sightings of a 300-foot craft hovering silently above ground. That's hard to dismiss."

He says he found the progression of events in Fyffe very interesting.

"These are small-town folks who are very open," he says. "We'd talk to one person, and end up with five more interviews out of one visit. For a while, I thought we would be talking to 100 people before we were through. Then "Inside Edition" threw a wet blanket over everything. Their report was so silly. You wouldn't believe the effect it had. It changed the town's whole attitude. People got suspicious and defensive, and began to clam up with any outsider."

According to Ballard, MUFON has three categories for UFO sightings — military aircraft that may be experimental; stars or planets; visitors from other worlds.

"There's the distinct possibility we're being visited by aliens," he says.

Admitting such a prospect is unnerving and exciting at the same time, he says he's not alone in feeling that way.

"I don't know what it was," says Donna Saylor. "I'm swaying between the possibility our government is experimenting with something, and visitors from outer space. I don't rule out intelligent life from other planets. I have a harder time not giving that theory some credit, because of the unusual circumstances around here."

She says the sightings are still going on, but few people report them anymore.

"My attitude is that if everyone hides it for fear of ridicule, we'll never get any answers," she reasons. "If lots of people report it, the authorities have got to investigate."

Chief Garmany has mixed feelings, too.

"No one was able to explain what me and Fred saw," he says. "I still say it's a UFO, and nobody has been able to explain it away."

Garmany believes that, while hysteria may have resulted in some of the unsubstantiated sightings, the majority of the people who called his station really saw a UFO.

"I think they might have seen aircraft or something man-made in some instances," he says. "The reports were so numerous at one time, we couldn't confirm all of them. I believe the people that called us really saw something, but in some cases our situation probably turned their heads toward the skies, and they might have seen objects they really didn't see or couldn't explain."

As a Fyffe businessman pointed out, a UFO is a flying object that is unidentified or unusual in its actions or flight pattern. Fyffe's flying object certainly fit that definition.

One thing is for sure. The people around Fyffe watch the skies a lot more these days. Like others who have had such encounters, they continue to monitor the heavens on clear nights, as if drawn by some invisible force.

"Once you see something like that, you don't ever quit watching the skies," says Mrs. Saylor. "When I'm traveling at night, if I'm not driving, I'm looking out the window and up at the skies. I'm fascinated by what might be up there."

(The people of Fyffe) are not backward country hicks who have drunk too much of their own moonshine. They are sober, literate, hard-working people who saw some strange sights that they cannot fully explain.

Who Killed
The Cows?

January 9, 1993, started like any other winter morning on Sand Mountain. The trees were stark and bare, their branches reaching toward the sky in silent supplication for the spring that seemed so far away.

Tommy Cole could not see the trees when he looked out his farmhouse window. Even though it was 8 a.m., the gray morning still enshrouded the landscape and the out-buildings in its misty cape.

"Time to check on the cattle," Cole thought to himself, as he drained the last drop of coffee from his cup.

During the week, the livestock responsibility was handled by hired hands. But this was Saturday, Cole was off work, and the farm chores fell to him and his wife. Cole did not mind, though.

He loved the lifestyle he led, as chief detective of the Albertville Police Department Monday through Friday, and cattle rancher on the weekends.

Being in law enforcement, he really did not get off

at 5 p.m. on Fridays, even though Albertville was a quiet little town and not subject to the rash of rapes, robberies and burglaries of big cities. Still, he had time to savor his wife's biscuits and gravy on weekends, and to linger over that second cup of coffee in his own comfortable kitchen.

Winters are mild throughout most of Alabama, but on Sand Mountain, in the northeastern part of the state, wind chill factors can make your bones feel like an Arctic ice floe. A blast of cold air reminded Cole of this fact as soon as he stepped outside his back door. The cold did not shock him, but what he found 300 yards from his house did, and his life has not been the same since.

"I went to feed my steers and realized I was one short," recalls Cole. "I thought maybe a coyote had gotten to him, but when I found him, I realized no wild animal could have killed that steer."

There were no torn body parts strewn around, no bloody tracks, none of the evidence normally left behind when predators attack. But it did not require a detective to determine that something was missing. The steer's sexual organs were gone, as well as his rectum. Not ripped out in the feeding frenzy of some wild beast of prey, but cut with the surgical precision of a two-legged animal who knew his way around with a sharp instrument.

Something else was odd about this case, too, Cole thought as he examined the carcass. His subconscious mind picked up on it before the truth seared his consciousness—there was no blood.

Zilch. Zero. None at the wounds, none on the body, none on the ground around the animal. And, he was to find later, none inside the body either. It was as if a vampire had struck during the night, snipped off certain organs, cauterized the wounds and drained the body dry.

Cole shivered, then went back inside his house to

make a phone call. Waiting for his veterinarian to arrive, he tried to recall any unusual noises he might have heard the night before.

He had slept like a baby, though, and no sounds other than his wife's snoring so much as tickled the hairs in his ears before the morning sun stroked his cheeks.

Suddenly, Cole remembered the crazy question his wife had asked on Thursday morning.

"She wanted to know why a helicopter would be in our pasture," Cole says. "I asked her whether she had been drinking kerosene."

When Cole's vet told him the steer probably had been dead a couple of days, something clicked in Cole's mind, and he began talking to his neighbors.

"Two of them described the same color and type helicopter my wife described when I talked sensibly to her," Cole says.

He learned about other incidents, starting the previous October, where cows, goats and at least one dog were found under similar circumstances, dead in their pastures, with various body parts removed. As with his own steer, the wounds were surgically precise cuts, with no evidence of ripping and tearing. In some instances, the animals had been drained of their blood, and in every case, there were no traces of automobile tracks, footprints, or blood around the site. All of the strange killings took place within four miles of Albertville.

As more mutilated animals were discovered, strange theories begin to circulate. Some said it was the work of devil worshippers carrying out their satanic rites. People in adjoining DeKalb County reported hearing strange noises and seeing bright lights in the sky, giving rise to speculation of UFO involvement.

But as farmers compared notes, a very real and disturbing pattern emerged. Unmarked, unlighted helicopters were seen or heard at almost all of the mutilation sites the night before carcasses were found.

"I saw helicopters land in my pasture one night," John Strawn, a farmer with 30 head of cattle, worth about $12,000, told a newspaper reporter. Strawn organized other farmers, who, on various occasions, were able to identify three turbine helicopters. One was light blue and white with an orange sun painted on it, one was dark blue, and the other was black.

One night, a helicopter hovered so close to a woman's trailer that it vibrated the dishes off her kitchen shelves. When she looked out her window, she saw that the helicopter had herded several of her neighbor's cows into a corner of his pasture, and was shining a spotlight on them.

Several Sand Mountain residents got together and decided they would shoot down the next mysterious helicopter they saw.

Keith Gilbreath, a satellite dish retailer and installer who lives near several of the mutilation sites, says they wanted to interrogate any survivors. But Ben Gamel, who was sheriff of Marshall County at the time, says that would have been a big mistake.

"The National Guard stages exercises with their helicopters over Sand Mountain every week," Gamel says. "I see them, I hear them, I know what a Huey sounds like. I told one farmer it would have been awful if he had shot down a military 'copter and killed the four innocent people aboard because he thought they mutilated his cattle."

Meanwhile, state investigators dismissed the livestock killings as the work of predators and scavengers.

"There is no evidence whatsoever, or the slightest suggestion toward satanic activity," James Miller, an investigator for the state Department of Agriculture, said after looking into 14 of the bovine deaths. The helicopter and UFO reports offered "no direct evidence to link them with any animal deaths," and only one death may have been a mutilation, he said.

An 18-year veteran of law enforcement, Miller put the blame on coyotes, wild dogs and vultures. Dr. Danny Thrash, a DeKalb County veterinarian, agreed. He saw two of the dead cattle, and both appeared to have been eaten by coyotes or buzzards.

"If there's something going on, I think it has been exaggerated," Thrash told newspaper reporters.

State Agriculture Commissioner A.W. Todd, claiming the animals died of natural causes, said his department could not find anything amiss in the killings. Livestock often die in the field, and many are partially eaten by predators. Teeth marks can be hidden as the body decomposes and swells, leaving the appearance of "a clean cut," he said.

The mutilations caught the attention of Fyffe police officer Ted Oliphant. Fyffe had been the site of a highly publicized string of UFO sightings in 1989, so it was only natural for the UFO angle to interest him.

Publicly proclaiming a state cover-up, Oliphant personally investigated 35 mutilations reported between October, 1991, and April, 1993. Predatory animals were responsible for only three cases. In the other 32 cases, oval-shaped cuts were found on many of the animals, and the same body parts were almost always removed.

Oliphant called in some investigators of his own, including a Colorado pathologist. Tests from tissue samples from one of the dead animals showed it had been burned with temperatures exceeding 300 degrees, and a strange chemical combination was found on another.

"I have no idea what's doing it to these animals, but I think we should find out," Oliphant said at the time.

Chief Det. Tommy Cole smelled the same rat as Oliphant. He and the other farmers who had lost cattle could not reconcile the official reports with the evidence before their own eyes.

"I've seen a lot in my 31 years in law enforcement, but I've never seen anything like this," Cole says. "I've been called out on several different occasions where I had to tell farmers it was predators that got their cows. I could tell by the way the animals were torn or pulled, and parts of the animals strewn about. But where specific parts were taken, with smooth, precision cuts, this was different. The sheriff, state officials... there's got to be a cover-up, but I don't know why."

Cole does not buy into the UFO theory. "What I saw was helicopters, strange helicopters with no I.D. numbers or letters.

"I saw real live people in some of them, too. When they realized someone was watching them, they flew off."

One night, Cole saw three different helicopters in one area, each chopper the same dark blue with a smattering of gray on its sides. Although there were none of the FAA-required I.D. markings, Cole did notice the words "Bell Jet Ranger" on each of them. He even got some FAA officials to watch the skies with him on one occasion, and they, too, scratched their heads over the low-flying whirlybirds.

"There was no evidence that the choppers landed at any of the mutilation sites, but who says they did?" Cole asks. "They could have gotten close enough to dart the cows with dart guns, then stepped off the choppers. All of the places I investigated had many cattle in the pastures. A lot of the cattle had been around those dead cows, and they would have tromped out any human footprints. Believe me, I looked at every angle."

Cole scoffs at the notion that predators were responsible for the mutilations.

"I've never seen coyotes fly helicopters," he says, without a trace of humor in his voice.

None of the other farmers agreed with the state's official explanation, either. Buck Armstrong, who found one of his cows mutilated in April, 1993, said no coyote could have neatly removed the animal's udder or cut a clean, 12-inch hole in its back.

"There wasn't any predatory animals around; no tracks or nothing," Armstrong said. "I've had cattle that predators got to. It's not predators."

Margaret Pope of nearby Geraldine agreed. She found one of her cows dead with the udder cut off, too. "It looked like a cookie-cutter cut," she said.

So if it was not predators, Satanists, or UFOs, what was it?

Some, including Guntersville resident Keith Gilbreath, swear it was the United States Government. Gilbreath says that for about a year prior to the mutilations, he had frequently heard the drone of a C-130 cargo plane over his farm between 8:30 and 11:30 at night. Usually alone but occasionally in pairs, the planes would fly so low that Gilbreath could see the cargo doors open beneath the tails. Being a former military man, he figured out quickly why the planes were flying so low.

"They were down below radar, in between Sand Mountain and what I call Gilbreath Ridge, because the Gilbreath family settled a lot of that land over there," he says.

He knew from experience that when a C-130's cargo door opens, it is usually an indication the plane is about to make a drop. Although puzzled, he dismissed the planes from his mind until the cattle mutilations began.

"I asked myself why they would be flying so long before these cattle mutilations started," Gilbreath says. "I said, well, they could be flying in supplies. But what for? Then I thought about the helicopters. You see, the refueling range for a Bell Jet Ranger is 300 to 400 miles. Someone checked every place a helicopter could refuel within 300 miles of Marshall and DeKalb counties, and no one reported refueling any helicopters or doing any maintenance or seeing any helicopters of that type near the dates the cattle mutilations occurred. So I said, well, there's only one answer for that. If the helicopters aren't being refueled and they're not flying to a base anywhere, obviously they're still here."

Gilbreath figured the cargo planes were servicing and refueling the helicopters over Lake Guntersville State Park, a very large, rugged, unpopulated area full of deep, dark canyons.

Then it dawned on him that there might be an even greater connection between the cargo planes and the cattle mutilations.

If specimens were being collected, he reasoned, they would have to be taken out of the area quickly. Could the C-130s be making some in-flight pickups, perhaps?

"There is a technique where C-130s can take objects up in the air without landing," says Gilbreath. "I saw 'em do it in Vietnam."

Gilbreath has formed an interesting theory as to the government's reasons for collecting bovine body parts, and for stealing from farmers on Sand Mountain instead of buying the cattle they needed. He thinks that during the Cuban Missile Crisis of 1962, the government may have sought a secret, out-of-the-way place to store nuclear weapons or weapons-grade plutonium. Officials wanted to get it away from the Florida military bases, which were well-known to the Cubans and Russians, he thinks. Once the crisis had passed, the whereabouts of the stash could have been forgotten until the military detected a high amount of ground radiation when flying over Sand Mountain.

"If weapons-grade plutonium was stored underground, it could have leaked into the ground water, and that could be deadly," says Gilbreath. "It can go for miles and miles on the surface of the ground, and it can contaminate everything, humans, dogs, cattle, everything."

What started that line of thinking was the death of Gilbreath's father and several of his father's hunting buddies, all within a very short time of each other. The elder Gilbreath died of a rare form of liver cancer, and several of his buddies, including a cousin, died of cancer, too.

"They were all about the same age, and they all did quail hunting, which has to cover a lot of ground," Gilbreath explains.

"My dad went all over Sand Mountain and other places hunting. I got to thinking that maybe weapons-grade plutonium could have leaked into the soil on Sand Mountain, and that my dad and his buddies picked it up because they walked the mountain so much."

Having read a lot about the accident at the Chernobyl nuclear plant in Russia, Gilbreath thought of other radioactive elements that might be the villains in this scenario. He learned that cesium and radioactive iodine are the first elements that show up in the ground soil following a nuclear leak or explosion.

He also learned that cows were the first animals checked by Russians investigating the Chernobyl fall-out. Then he noticed a parallel to the way the cattle on Sand Mountain were mutilated.

"They cut the jaws out of the cows, because that's where the cow first ingests the grass," he says, speaking of the Russians.

"They checked the mouth area for residue, and the milk sack, or udder, for any residue that might be left in processing the milk. The anus is the last place that the material would be processed. It also settles in the genitals of a male animal."

Gilbreath believes the only other source that could cause that kind of radiation would be an accidental drop of an unarmed nuclear device from a U.S. military aircraft.

"It could have buried itself in the ground, and

maybe they knew the general area but they didn't know exactly where it was," he theorizes again. "And maybe they've been testing this area for years to see how bad the plutonium is leaking. That's my only other theory. I can't think of any other reason on this earth why this would have happened."

Former Sheriff Ben Gamel thinks the idea of governmental involvement is, well, a bunch of hogwash.

"I talked to people who were actually involved in the mutilations," says Gamel, a retired state trooper. "They were in jail at the time, and they told me how it was done and why. There were actually two unconnected groups involved. We investigated, but they had covered their tracks pretty well, so we couldn't prove it. They wouldn't sign any statements, and we needed corroborating evidence to charge them. But I have no doubt that what they told me was true, because they even told me where they did it, and the carcasses were there. The ones who controlled it cut it off because things were getting too hot."

Gamel says he cannot reveal who the culprits were, or their reasons, because it may hamper any future investigations.

As talkative as Keith Gilbreath was at first, the Sand Mountain farmers began to clam up when they realized they were being scoffed at. The sheriff in neighboring DeKalb County reportedly told his employees they were not to discuss mutilations or UFOs anymore. Adding to the mystery, the state veterinarian involved in the case resigned. So did Sheriff Gamel, although he says it had nothing to do with the mutilations.

The last reported mutilation was in February, 1994, 16 months after the first. Like the others, it was never solved.

Some people around Albertville still watch for helicopters occasionally, and a few still talk in hushed tones about UFOs and Satanists. Like Gilbreath, Detective Cole has his own ideas.

"My theory has to do with government experiments, too, but I can't tell you any more," Cole says. "Go rent the video, 'Endangered Species,' and you'll know what I'm talking about."

"Endangered Species" is based on a true story of cattle mutilations that took place in a western state several years ago.

It, too, points to covert government experiments as the explanation.

"It's unbelievable," Cole says.

Acknowledgments

This book could not have been written without the help of many people. I would like to express my heartfelt gratitude to those who took time from their busy schedules to talk to a total stranger over the telephone; to those who stuck their necks out and gave me their opinions; to those who allowed me to quote them; to those who supplied me with the fruits of their own research; and to those who had no information to offer but knew someone who did.

Most of those people are mentioned by name within individual chapters. Others remain in the background, but played important roles in my research. They include:

• The staff of the Southern History Department at the Birmingham Public Library, who spent several hours with me on the premises and over the telephone;

• The staff of the Local History and Genealogy Division of the Mobile Public Library, particularly George Schroeter, division head;

• John Hatcher Jackson III, who supplied me with the wonderfully sentimental letters his great-great grandfather wrote to his great-great grandmother during the Civil War;

• Linda Derry, project manager and site archeologist for the Cahawba Project, who supplied tips and material on legends of the Selma area;

• Julie Lyons, archeologist for the Cahawba Project, who encouraged her father to share his tale of the Wampus Cat, and who accompanied us on an after-dark tour of the creature's territory;

• The volunteers at the Bessemer Hall of History, who graciously allowed me access to their files and their memories;

- A.J. Wright, clinical librarian, UAB Department of Anesthesiology Library, who furnished me with articles he wrote on Railroad Bill and other outlaws;
- Neil Collier, Alger-Sullivan Historical Society, Century, Florida, who collected a thick file on Railroad Bill; and Neil's wife, Sandy, who photocopied it for me;
- Joey Brackner, folklorist, Alabama State Council on the Arts, who encouraged me and supplied me with several leads;
- The staff of the Choctaw County Library;
- Tom Taylor, retired executive editor, *Mobile Press Register*, and the *Press Register* librarian.

I am especially grateful to my older daughter, Heather, for proofreading the drafts of these chapters and offering her editorial comments; to my younger daughter, Amanda, who rarely complained when I would get so wrapped up in this book that I would forget to pick her up from school; to my husband, Jack, who supported me emotionally and financially throughout this project; to my mother, Doris Wilson, who kept my house clean so I could work; and to my good friends and fellow authors, Lynn Grisard Fullman and Kathryn Murray, who lifted me up when this project threatened to get me down.

In addition to those named, dozens of other people pointed me toward leads and legends that, for one reason or another, did not pan out in time for this book. To them I say: Your time was not wasted. I may have enough material for another one!

—EHM

Photo by Jesse Ducoté

About The Author

Elaine Hobson Miller was born, raised and educated in Birmingham, Alabama, where she received her BA in journalism from Samford University. She was the first female reporter to cover the City Hall beat for the *Birmingham Post-Herald*, and later worked as a food editor and features writer for the morning daily. She also worked as a staff writer for *Birmingham Magazine*.

As a free-lance writer, her byline has appeared in *The Birmingham News*, *Business Alabama Monthly*, *Alabama Magazine*, *Woman's World*, and numerous national trade publications. She is president of Alabama Media Professionals and a member of the National Federation of Press Women.

When she's not writing, she's riding her horse, Jager, or watching a British mystery on television. She lives in Birmingham with her husband and two daughters.

This is her first book.